5

Wm James
22-23
Psa susceptible
to controlled
experience §1

A Godless Jew

BOOKS BY PETER GAY

The Bourgeois Experience: Victoria to Freud,
volume II, The Tender Passion (1986)

Freud for Historians (1985)

The Bourgeois Experience: Victoria to Freud,
volume I, Education of the Senses (1984)

Freud, Jews and Other Germans: Masters and Victims
in Modernist Culture (1978)

Art and Act: On Causes in History—Manet, Gropius, Mondrian (1976)

Style in History (1974)

Modern Europe (1973), with R. K. Webb

The Bridge of Criticism: Dialogues on the Enlightenment (1970)

The Enlightenment: An Interpretation,
volume II, The Science of Freedom (1969)

Weimar Culture: The Outsider as Insider (1968)

A Loss of Mastery: Puritan Historians in Colonial America (1966)

The Enlightenment: An Interpretation,
volume I, The Rise of Modern Paganism (1966)

The Party of Humanity: Essays in the French Enlightenment (1964)

Voltaire's Politics: The Poet as Realist (1959)

The Dilemma of Democratic Socialism:
Eduard Bernstein's Challenge to Marx (1952)

❀ A Godless Jew

Freud, Atheism, and the Making of Psychoanalysis

Peter Gay

YALE UNIVERSITY PRESS, NEW HAVEN AND LONDON

IN ASSOCIATION WITH

HEBREW UNION COLLEGE PRESS, CINCINNATI

Designed by Sally Harris
and set in Garamond type by
Brevis Press, Bethany, Connecticut
Printed in the United States of America by
Vail-Ballou Press, Binghamton, N.Y.

Library of Congress Cataloging-in-Publication Data

Gay, Peter, 1923–
  A Godless Jew.

  Bibliography: p.
  Includes index.
    1. Freud, Sigmund, 1856–1939—Religion.
2. Psychoanalysis and religion.   3. Atheism.
I. Title.
BF173.F85G38   1987   150.19'52   87–8267
ISBN 0–300–04008–3

The paper in this book meets the guidelines for
permanence and durability of the Committee on
Production Guidelines for Book Longevity
of the Council on Library Resources.

10   9   8   7   6   5   4   3   2   1

The Gustave A. and Mamie W. Efroymson Memorial Lectures
delivered at the Hebrew Union College-Jewish Institute of Religion
in Cincinnati, Ohio, during December 1986

For
Hank Gibbons

fellow enthusiast, fellow skeptic

Quite by the way, why did none of the devout create psychoanalysis?
Why did one have to wait for a completely godless Jew?
—Sigmund Freud to Oskar Pfister, October 9, 1918

CONTENTS

PREFACE AND ACKNOWLEDGMENTS   xi

A NOTE ON TRANSLATIONS AND ABBREVIATIONS   xv

INTRODUCTION
Science against Religion: "Clericalism, There's the Enemy"   1

ONE
The Last Philosophe: "Our God Logos"   35

TWO
In Search of Common Ground: "A Better Christian Never Was"   69

THREE
The Question of a Jewish Science: "A Title of Honor"   115

BIBLIOGRAPHY   157

INDEX   179

PREFACE AND ACKNOWLEDGMENTS

This book grew out of the Gustave A. and Mamie W. Efroymson Memorial Lectures I delivered at Hebrew Union College in Cincinnati on December 1, 4, and 8, 1986. I have added some illustrative material, footnotes, a bibliographical essay, and an introductory chapter, but for the rest the text transcribes the lectures as I gave them. I had a single argument to make, and have found that the informal mode of presentation suited it best, even in print.

The theme of these lectures may seem surprising for a theological seminary. To be sure, theologians have for centuries enjoyed debating the unbeliever, to sharpen their dialectical skills or, perhaps, to gather kindling for the stake awaiting the unrepentant heretic. But there are other, and I think more cogent, reasons for reflecting at a theological seminary on Freud's atheism and on its meaning for his creation, psychoanalysis. The historical tension between science and religion is far more intricate than most believers, or unbelievers, have recognized. As we shall see, Freud himself was one who failed to do justice to these intricacies. And some who were close to him, members of his own family, were less than clear about Freud's own position. His nephew Harry Freud, for one, even denied him the status of an atheist. Others, equally close to him or even closer, like his daughter Anna, have argued that psychoanalysis is a Jewish creation. Such conflicts of testimony and interpretations abound. I have written this book to help resolve them.

I found it a singular pleasure to write, and to deliver, these lectures. It seems invidious to single out a few of those who made our week on the campus of Hebrew Union College so agreeable, but I want particularly to mention Professor Michael J. Cook, chairman of the Efroymson Lectureship Committee, who took kind charge of us from the moment we reached the Cincinnati airport to the moment we returned to it, and who smoothed our way by taking care of every possible detail. Professor Michael A. Meyer asked the right questions and has left his mark on the text. Fred and Dee Gottschalk, president of Hebrew Union College and his wife, made our visit a memorable one.

I drafted the first version of this book in the summer of 1986, in the fostering atmosphere of Churchill College, Cambridge, England, and received some much-needed support both technical and moral from old friends and new: Stefan Collini and Ruth Morse, Jay and Tami Winter, Quentin Skinner and Susan James, Harold James and Steven Beller, and Wallace MacCaffrey. I want to thank Mark Paterson of the Sigmund Freud Archives, Wivenhoe, ably assisted by Jo Richardson, for easing my way into their Freud treasures and for permission to quote from them. I am indebted to Pearl King, Honorary Archivist of the British Psycho-Analytical Society, London, for permission to quote from the Anna Freud-Ernest Jones correspondence, and Jill Duncan, Executive Officer of the Archives, for her assistance; to David L. Newlands, Curator of the Freud Museum, London, and Steve Neufeld for an exceptionally gracious reception (only underscored by our correspondence) and permission to quote from their Freud holdings. I want also to thank Dr. Ronald S. Wilkinson, Manuscript Division, Library of Congress, for courteous and effective help in my searches in the magnificent Freud Collection. Dr. Anna K. Wolff kindly allowed me to quote from a letter of Freud's to her father, Ernst Kris. I am grateful as well to my old friend Bob Webb for timely help, and Jim Lochart for his assistance. My old friend Gladys Topkis proved, not surprisingly, a thoughtful and generous editor, and the sharp-eyed copyediting by Lawrence Kenney preserved me from some mistakes I should not have made. My wife, Ruth, did not merely hear but also (as always to my great benefit) read each of the chapters as they came along. I am grateful to her. I am grateful, too, to my friend Hank Gibbons, to whom I have dedicated this book. He will know why.

A NOTE ON TRANSLATIONS
AND ABBREVIATIONS

All translations from Freud's writings and letters are my own
(as are virtually all the other translations), though I have consulted, and benefited from, the work of other translators. Since
the principal audience for this book is bound to be English-
speaking, I have, for my readers' convenience, cited both the
original version I used and (in parentheses) the page numbers
of available English-language editions.

Abbreviations

Briefe: Sigmund Freud, *Briefe 1873–1939,* ed. Ernst L. and
Lucie Freud (1960; 2d enlarged ed., 1968). English version,
Letters of Sigmund Freud, 1873–1939, tr. Tania and James Stern
(1975).

Freud-Abraham: Sigmund Freud, Karl Abraham, *Briefe
1907–1926,* ed. Hilda C. Abraham and Ernst L. Freud
(1965). English version, *A Psycho-Analytic Dialogue: The Letters
of Sigmund Freud and Karl Abraham, 1907–1926,* tr. Bernard
Marsh and Hilda C. Abraham (1965).

Freud-Fliess: Sigmund Freud. Briefe an Wilhelm Fliess, 1887–1904. Ungekürzte Ausgabe, ed. Jeffrey Moussaieff Masson; German version by Michael Schröter, transcriptions by Gerhard Fichtner (1986). English version, *The Complete Letters of Sigmund Freud to Wilhelm Fliess, 1887–1904,* tr. Jeffrey Moussaieff Masson (1985).

Freud-Jung: Sigmund Freud/C. G. Jung. Briefwechsel, ed. William McGuire and Wolfgang Sauerländer (1974). English version, *The Freud/Jung Letters,* tr. Ralph Manheim (Freud's letters) and R. F. C. Hull (Jung's letters) (1974).

Freud-Pfister: Sigmund Freud, Oskar Pfister, *Briefe 1909–1939,* ed. Ernst L. Freud and Heinrich Meng (1963). English version, *Psycho-Analysis and Faith: The Letters of Sigmund Freud and Oskar Pfister,* tr. Eric Mosbacher (1963).

GW: Sigmund Freud, *Gesammelte Werke,* 18 vols., ed. Anna Freud with the collaboration of Marie Bonaparte, E. Bibring, W. Hoffer, E. Kris, and O. Isakower (1940–52).

Int. Jl. of Psycho-Anal.: International Journal of Psycho-Analysis.

Int. Rev. of Psycho-Anal.: International Review of Psycho-Analysis.

Int. Z. für Psychoanal.: Internationale Zeitschrift für (ärztliche) Psychoanalyse.

Jones I, II, III: Ernest Jones, *The Life and Work of Sigmund Freud,* 3 vols. Vol. I, *The Formative Years and the Great Discoveries, 1856–1900* (1953). Vol. II, *Years of Maturity, 1901–1919* (1955). Vol. III, *The Last Phase, 1919–1939* (1957).

LC: Library of Congress, Washington, D.C.

Protokolle: Herman Nunberg and Ernst Federn, eds., *Proto-*

kolle der Wiener Psychoanalytischen Vereinigung, 4 vols. (1976–81). English version, *Minutes of the Vienna Psychoanalytic Society* (1962–75).

SE: The Standard Edition of the Complete Psychological Works of Sigmund Freud, 24 vols., ed. James Strachey, tr. in collaboration with Anna Freud, assisted by Alix Strachey and Alan Tyson (1953–74).

�֍ INTRODUCTION

Science against Religion:

"Clericalism, There's the Enemy"

In one of his papers on technique, Freud tells a delicious story about an insurance agent and a pastor. He intended it as a cautionary tale against therapists making compromises with their austere technique, but it illuminates, quite incidentally, the strength, the sheer exuberance, of his atheism. At the instance of his anxious and pious family, a mortally ill insurance agent allows a pastor to call on him. The family's hope is that the pastor may persuade the dying man, a convinced unbeliever, to make his peace with God. Their private talk lasts so long that the family, waiting outside, begins to hope for the patient's conversion. "At last, the door of the sick room opens," Freud concludes. "The unbeliever has not been converted, but the pastor goes away insured."[1]

Freud in fact advertised his unbelief every time he could find, or make, an opportunity. But, tellingly enough, many have chosen to ignore this self-definition. The skeptics include even a member of his own family. "Sigmund Freud consciously felt himself a Jew, but he was thoroughly antireligious, though not by any means an atheist," his nephew Harry Freud told an

1. "Bemerkungen über die Übertragungsliebe" (1915), *GW* X, 314 / "Observations on Transference Love," *SE* XII, 165.

interviewer in 1956. "It is just that he did not think much of
rites and dogmas."[2] If even someone fairly close to him can
find the boldness to contradict Freud's explicit testimony and,
for that matter, the overwhelming evidence, it is no wonder
that interpretations of Freud's Judaism and, more broadly, the
relationship between psychoanalysis and religion have prolif-
erated and diverged across the years. The conflicts in which
readers of Freud have become enmeshed have left unanswered
some interesting questions about Freud's mind and about the
essential nature of psychoanalysis. I have written this book to
address them and to propose some resolutions.

These questions grow no more manageable for being embed-
ded in the largest possible framework, the tangled history of
the traffic between religion and science from the days of Newton
onward. Freud himself, it must be admitted, did his part to
compound, or at least not disentangle, these complexities. In
his confident comments on the evolution of the scientific world
view to which he was so firmly attached, he found himself, as
he rarely did, on the side of the conventional wisdom. In Eu-
ropean-Christian culture, he observed, "religion no longer has
the same influence on people that it used to have." This shift
toward secularism had come about not because the "promises
of religion" had grown smaller, but because they appear less
"credible" to the twentieth-century mind. One powerful, and
Freud thought really quite obvious, moving force of this modern skepticism was "the strengthening of the scientific spirit
in the higher strata of human society." Freud visualized the

2. Harry Freud in Richard Dyck, "Mein Onkel Sigmund," *Aufbau,*
May 11, 1956, p. 3.

confrontation of religion and science as one of pure and permanent animosity. "Criticism has gnawed away at the probative power of religious documents; natural science has shown up the errors they contain; comparative research has been struck by the fatal resemblance of the religious conceptions we revere to the mental products of primitive peoples and times."[3]

Freud visualized this secularization as a slow, tormented, but in the end extremely dramatic evolution. "The scientific spirit generates a certain posture toward matters of this world; before matters of religion it stops for a while, hesitates, at last there too crosses the threshold. In this process there is no stopping; the more the treasures of our knowledge become accessible to people, the more the defection from religious belief will spread, at first only from its obsolete, offensive vestments, but then from its fundamental presuppositions as well."[4] Still, in offering this historical overview Freud displays a certain caution; he was happy to claim, with other commentators, impressive advances for the troops of secularism, but he refused to commit himself to easy optimism. Victory was not yet at hand. "The struggle of the scientific spirit against the religious world view," he wrote, looking back in 1932, "has not come to an end; it is still going on in the present before our eyes."[5]

Appraisals of this sort had been commonplaces among critics and historians of culture even before Freud's time. Certainly

3. *Die Zukunft einer Illusion,* GW XIV, 361–62 / *The Future of an Illusion,* SE XXI, 38.

4. Ibid., 362 / 38.

5. "Über eine Weltanschauung," *Neue Folge der Vorlesungen zur Einführung in die Psychoanalyse,* GW XV, 182 / "The Question of a Weltanschauung," *New Introductory Lectures on Psycho-Analysis,* SE XXII, 169.

the irrevocable divorce he decreed between science and religion was not new. The decades stretching from the French Revolution to the outbreak of the First World War resemble nothing so much as a vast battlefield strewn with timeworn creeds and modern heresies, and animated by the heroic antics of new sects. These metaphors, borrowed from military or sportive combat, are tired, rather shopworn, but I shall continue to use them throughout this book, for they efficiently convey the atmosphere and, even better, they echo the vocabulary of the combatants. Freud himself flatly called religion the "enemy." Inevitably, the word will appear often in these pages.

Freud was in good company. Two of the most characteristic and most popular polemical texts of the late nineteenth century, John William Draper's *History of the Conflict between Religion and Science* and Andrew Dickson White's *History of the Warfare of Science with Theology in Christendom,* encapsulate, in their incendiary titles, a deeply felt nineteenth-century perception. Even those who avoided the language of warfare saw themselves in a fight to the finish, a fight, moreover, that had been raging for many decades. In the summer of 1873—the year Freud entered the University of Vienna—one of the most intrepid soldiers in the army of secularism, T. H. Huxley, wrote to his wife, "The part I have to play is not to found a new school of thought or to reconcile the antagonisms of the old school. We are in the midst of a gigantic movement greater than that which preceded and produced the Reformation, and really only the continuation of that movement." The ideas "at the bottom of the movement" were anything but new, but this much seemed plain to him: no "reconcilement" was "possible between free thought and traditional authority. One or other will have to succumb after a struggle of unknown duration." Huxley had every confidence that his side, "free thought," organizing "human life and the world as one harmonious whole," would "win in the long run." But he believed, too, that before the final defeat of authority, the world would see "vast political and social troubles."[6] Plainly, bellicose language seemed apt to contemporaries.

This war, to be sure, was punctuated by truces; it saw compromises no less than confrontations. But the confrontations were ever renewed because the compromises rarely produced acceptable and lasting settlements. The nineteenth century was arguably more pious, certainly more churchgoing, than the eighteenth. This held especially true for the respectable classes. "Most of the educated people of our time (as distinct from the uncultured masses)," the widely read German Social Darwinist and anticlerical polemicist Ernst Haeckel noted at the end of the century, "remain in the conviction that religion is a separate branch of our mental life, independent of science, and not less valuable and indispensable."[7] William James had been suggesting the validity of such a division of labor for some years. But sizable pockets of anticlericalism and of secularist contempt for all religion were scattered across the map of European culture. They were probably most visible in France, but everywhere Christianity had to record some spectacular defections,

6. T. H. Huxley to his wife, August 8, 1873. Leonard Huxley, ed., *Life and Letters of Thomas Henry Huxley*, 2 vols. (1900), I, 397.

7. Haeckel, *The Riddle of the Universe* (1899; tr. Joseph McCabe, 1900), 339.

especially after Darwin. Edmund Gosse's moving autobiography, *Father and Son,* with its famous report on his loss of belief in defiance of his father's pathetic fundamentalism, is only the best-known history of many nineteenth-century desertions from the faith. But unbelievers faced counterattacks from the devout; the many who had never wavered were joined by those who returned to the saving shelter of belief, or at least to a conviction of its utility. The unsettling upheavals of the French Revolution, followed by its no less unsettling Napoleonic aftermath, proved persuasive recruiting sergeants for piety.

The participants in these struggles well understood that the stakes were high. Biologists, pedagogues, journalists, politicians, all were deeply immersed in battle. Wherever the historian looks, he discovers tensions over the nature of God and the powers of churches during the decades in which Freud was growing up, going to the university, establishing himself as a physician, and developing psychoanalysis. Interesting traces of those tensions seeped into the household of his parents, as his father, Jacob Freud, gradually emancipated himself from the faith of his ancestors. Those frightened by political and social change chose to equate liberal theology with atheism, and atheism with revolutionary Jacobinism. Unbelief carried the stigma, and the force, of subversion.

But the armies of devotion did not wholly prevail; they could stem the flood tide of secularism but never quite stop it. The signals pointed confusingly in contradictory directions. Partisans of religion might adduce vigorous missions at home and abroad or numerous papal encyclicals intervening in all aspects of life to suggest that religion was still very much alive. But their impious adversaries could interpret the same evidence in their own favor: missions only underscored the alienation of the masses, or of foreign cultures, from Christianity; papal activity was a sympton of desperation. Continued high church attendance by the middle classes was less ambiguous proof that atheism had not yet triumphed. Yet militant unbelievers had much heartening material to sustain their morale: the lack of faith endemic among many natural scientists, the angry anticlerical and antireligious propaganda emanating from Socialists and from radical bourgeois publicists and politicians. Léon Gambetta, one of the founders of the Third French Republic, eloquently spoke for the party of science when he characterized "clericalism," in a famous remark, quite simply as "the enemy."

No wonder religious establishments were racked with defensive uneasiness. Proposals for doctrinal revision or ecclesiastical reform, however reasonable or modest, brought quick, testy rebuttals from the faithful unwilling to make any concessions to men infected in the slightest by the notorious doctrines of the Enlightenment. In the midst of all this intransigence, the mediator and the moderate had an ungrateful assignment. Liberal Anglicans met the stern reproaches of the High Church, Catholicizing Oxford movement within their ranks; Orthodox Jews were appalled by, and sturdily resisted, the innovations of Reform congregations eager to join Western Civilization and the nineteenth century at the same time. French liberal Catholics were repudiated and eventually stifled by the papacy for venturing to infuse their creed with touches of modern thought. In the Paris of 1830, the abbé Lammenais, maker of felicitous slogans, had proclaimed that God and liberty could be united and pronounced Catholic liberalism a viable creature. But as late as 1864, Pope Pius IX, who had briefly flirted with liberal ideas at his accession nearly two decades earlier, thought it necessary to issue his energetic Syllabus of Errors, that monument of resistance to modernity. The encyclical offered no surfaces to compromise; it condemned, in the most meticulous detail, positions ranging from latitudinarianism and liberalism to rationalism and communism.

As developments in Britain eloquently attest, the advance of the secular spirit was tortuous at best. It took long and hesitant decades for the religious and political establishment to enfranchise Dissenters, Roman Catholics, and eventually Jews, or open Oxford and Cambridge to students who did not subscribe to the Thirty-Nine Articles of the Anglican Church. Yet in Britain as elsewhere the heirs of the Enlightenment were on the march. Toward the end of the century the papacy itself felt obliged to acknowledge that liberalism, especially when it addressed sensitive issues of social welfare, was not wholly of the devil. A few years later, in 1908, Friedrich Naumann, the influential German pastor, legislator, and political leader, observed with a mixture of pride and resignation that people of his time had "a somewhat different imagination from those of earlier times." Indeed, "the new imagination has gone through the school of the natural sciences."[8]

But each territorial gain that secularism could record was hotly contested and often at least partially reversed. Christianity even captured (or in many cases never relinquished its hold

8. Naumann, *Form und Farbe* (1909), 28, quoted in John Cornell, "What is a religious painting?" (manuscript, 1986), 10.

advantage. While resistance to the secular way of thinking did not crumble, let alone vanish, more and more concessions to the secular spirit appeared politic. "Whoever has had an opportunity of becoming acquainted with the mental condition of the intelligent classes in Europe and America," John William Draper, scientist, medical administrator, and cultural historian, wrote triumphantly in 1874, "must have perceived that there is a great and rapidly increasing departure from the public religious faith, and that, while among the frank this divergence is not concealed, there is a far more extensive and far more dangerous secession, private and unacknowledged."[14] The very name of that spreading new cult, Christian Science, attested to the overpowering prestige that natural scientists were amassing. So did the announced aim of theosophy, which, in Madame Blavatsky's sweeping formulation, proclaimed itself to be nothing less than a synthesis of science, religion, and philosophy. "Among all the healthy symptoms that characterize this age," William James wrote in 1881, "I know no sounder one than the eagerness which theologians show to assimilate results of science, and to hearken to the conclusions of men of science about universal matters. One runs a better chance of being listened to today if one can quote Darwin and Helmholtz than if one can only quote Schleiermacher or Coleridge."[15]

Such attempts at reconciliation, or at least redefinitions of the great conflict, were not the exclusive property of troubled,

14. John William Draper, *History of the Conflict between Religion and Science* (1874), v.

15. William James, "Reflex Action and Theism" (1881), in *The Will to Believe and Other Essays in Popular Philosophy* (1897), 111.

on) a number of radicals: in several Western countries, Christian Socialists offered an appealing alternative to many men and women of good will sensitive to the ravages of industrial capitalism but imbued with the will to believe. While outspoken German Social Democratic leaders like August Bebel took every opportunity to attack religion, many of their comrades found the articulate, aggressive anticlericalism and atheism of the party at once politically unwise and morally offensive.[9] The spirited, usually pretentious, and woolly minded debates that highly cultivated Germans and Freud's fellow Austrians conducted at the turn of the century over the nature of the Soul and the need for belief in Higher Spiritual Powers should have put paid to the notion that the disenchanted scientific spirit now reigned supreme among the educated. Even France, land of the Revolution, saw a substantial Catholic revival among men of letters as the anticlerical Third Republic took shape.[10] Indecisive evolutions such as these prompted Freud to observe, much later, that the war between religion and science had not yet come to an end.

While Freud could not help recognizing the continuing hold of religion on his time and culture, he failed to do justice to the complexities I have just lightly sketched in. His stark vista of a historic confrontation in which educated atheists were

9. See esp. Owen Chadwick, *The Secularization of the European Mind in the Nineteenth Century* (1975), 78–86.

10. It is best described in Richard Griffiths, *The Reactionary Revolution: The Catholic Revival in French Literature, 1870–1914* (1966).

pitted against unlettered believers lacks the subtlety he lavished on his analysis of the neuroses. At moments he made a stab at finer discriminations: "It remains to be considered," he wondered out loud to the psychoanalyst Max Eitingon in 1927, "whether analysis *in itself* must really lead to the giving up of religion."[11] The following year he wrote to his "dear Marie," Princess Marie Bonaparte, "You are right: one is in danger of overestimating the frequency of an irreligious attitude among intellectuals. I get convinced of that just now on observing the reactions to my [*Future of an*] *Illusion*. That comes from the most varied drinks being offered under the name of 'religion,' with a minimal percentage of alcohol—really non-alcoholic; but they still get drunk on it." Freud could hardly contain his disdain for such weak heads. "The old drinkers were after all a respectable body." He thought that to get drunk on apple juice was nothing less than ridiculous.[12] That was amusing and perceptive, but Freud rarely attempted such a nuanced analysis of the warfare in which he was taking such a prominent and aggressive part.

In truth, like other large-scale and seemingly interminable conflicts, the nineteenth-century combat between religion and science was not just interrupted by the truces of which I have spoken but, at the same time, was complicated by its internecine squabbles, its tepid summer soldiers, and, most confusing of all, its ambivalent and inconsistent partisans. Many good bourgeois continued to profess their inherited religious

11. Freud to Eitingon, June 20, 1927. By permission of Sigmund Freud Copyrights, Wivenhoe.

12. Freud to Marie Bonaparte, March 19, 1928. *Jones* III, 447.

allegiances with undoubted sincerity while they accepted the impieties of geologists about the age of the earth and of biologists about the animal nature of man. These were the people who, witnessing the illness of a spouse or a child, would pray and send for the doctor in the same breath. "About the middle of this century," Friedrich Engels recalled late in life, "what struck every cultivated foreigner who set up his residence in England, was what they were then bound to consider the religious bigotry and stupidity of the English respectable middle class." To Engels and his friends, "all materialists, or, at least, very advanced free-thinkers," it "appeared inconceivable that almost all educated people in England should believe in all sorts of impossible miracles." Even the geologists, he noted in dismay, distorted "the facts of their science so as not to clash too much with the myths of the book of Genesis."[13] Engels was notoriously hard on the English middle classes; he could have collected similar instances among French or German or American bourgeois. Moreover, many had long believed that what is loosely called liberal religion was perfectly compatible with scientific research. But wherever encountered, in whatever form, the defensive tenacity that enabled the educated to believe in one compartment of their minds what seemed demonstrably absurd in others made it very difficult for any war correspondent reporting the great battles between science and religion to compose comprehensible dispatches.

With the passing decades, the spectacular advances of natural sciences and of medicine gave unbelief an undeniable

13. Engels, *Socialism: Utopian and Scientific* (Introduction to first English edition, 1892, tr. Edward Aveling, ed. 1935), 12.

or adroit, theologians riding the coattails of the sciences. The very authors whose combative titles I cited earlier—*Conflict between Religion and Science,* and *Warfare of Science and Theology*—unexpectedly offered themselves in the cause of accommodation. Draper saw the "antagonism" between religion and science as essentially political. The combat that defined his age, he argued, was "the continuation of a struggle that commenced when Christianity began to attain political power." The enemy, in short, was Roman Catholicism, power-hungry, obscurantist, bloodthirsty, intent on making martyrs to knowledge whenever it secured supremacy. "Roman Christianity and Science are recognized by their respective adherents as being absolutely incompatible," Draper proclaimed in reiterative, rhythmic periods; "they cannot exist together; one must yield to the other; mankind must make its choice—it cannot have both." He thought that Protestantism was in a far more favorable position. If the Protestant churches would only live up to Luther's maxim, if they would only recognize "the right of private interpretation of the Scriptures," which is the very "foundation of intellectual liberty," they would be reconciled to science.[16] A curious amalgam of pantheistic nature worshiper and reverent deist, Draper was not attacking religious faith itself. Indeed, even though his *Conflict between Religion and Science* acquired the distinction of being placed on the Index, he was not even attacking Christianity.[17]

16. *Conflict between Religion and Science,* 363–64.

17. Draper's biographer, Donald Fleming, epigrammatically encapsulates Draper's essential intentions in a sentence: Draper was "trying to save religion from itself." *John William Draper and the Religion of Science* (1950), 130.

Andrew Dickson White, for his part, was intent on discovering what is pernicious in the history of Christian practice so that he might rescue what is valuable. An eminent diplomat, university president, and historian, he knew everyone and, it seems, everything. The warfare whose history White was reciting in two massive volumes was fundamentally between bigotry and tolerance, dogmatism and flexibility. In his lifelong religious education, to which he devotes several expansive chapters in his autobiography, White allowed his experience to broaden his perspective; yet, he protests, "no hostility to religion found lodgment in my mind." Certainly "nothing like an attack upon Christianity itself, or upon anything vital to it, did I ever make."[18] White only wanted to champion the cause of free inquiry and to set people thinking. Then "they would more and more dwell on what is permanent in Christianity and less and less on what is transient; more and more on its universal truths, less and less upon the creeds, forms, and observances in which these gems are set." White came to believe that "what the world needed was more religion rather than less; more devotion to humanity and less preaching of dogmas."[19]

Arm and arm with Draper, White postulated a God of some sort and stood, hat reverently in hand, before the glorious mysteries of the universe. Like so many among the nineteenth-century troop carrying the banner of enlightenment, liberalism, and science, he and Draper were pervaded by the oceanic feeling of awe before the universe that Freud could not detect

18. *Autobiography*, 2 vols. (1905), II, 560.
19. Ibid., 561–62.

in himself. They cherished that undefinable sense of connect-
edness which Freud's acquaintance Romain Rolland took to be
at the heart of religious sentiments. Freud professed an interest
in analyzing that feeling but he did not really respect it. It
smacked of nonalcoholic apple juice working, like an unde-
tected placebo, to induce a state of religious intoxication. For
Freud, to be scientific meant to be sober.

If the popular account of the tension between science and
religion grossly oversimplified the intricacies of its history, a
widespread concurrent habit of mind brought still worse con-
fusion: the dilution of the term "religion" to a shallow, virtually
universal metaphor for any conviction firmly held and obstinately
defended. It was not in Freud's interest to support such facile
identifications. He had, after all, taken some pride in his claim
that it was "psychoanalysis which made the most recent contribution to the critique of the religious world view."[20] He was
no Marxist, but he agreed with the young Marx that "criticism
of religion is the premise of all criticism,"[21] and the criticism
of religion demanded the sharpest possible separation of science
from religion in whatever guise. But Freud was trapped by his
gift for vivid metaphor. He appealed to his "god logos" and
scattered other terms borrowed from theology through his vo-

20. "Über eine Weltanschauung," *Neue Folge der Vorlesungen, GW* XV,
180–81 / "Question of a Weltanschauung," *New Introductory Lectures, SE*
XXII, 167.

21. Introduction to "Contributions to the Critique of Hegel's Philosophy
of Right" (1844), in Robert C. Tucker, ed., *The Marx-Engels Reader* (1972;
2d ed., 1978), 53.

luminous writings. As a medical student, he glorified "our most modern saints, like Darwin, Haeckel, etc."[22] In the early 1880s, in a letter to his fiancée, he called Helmholtz, that Renaissance man of modern science, "one of my idols."[23] More damaging still, in 1899 he spoke to his friend Fliess about "the religion of science—*Wissenschaftsreligion*—which is supposed to have superseded the old religion."[24] Freud's most ardent supporters imitated him faithfully in this as in so much else. They would refer to analytic candidates as novices, think of Jung as a schismatic, detect in the meetings of the Vienna Psychoanalytic Society the pious atmosphere of a religious fraternity.

Yet for Freud, his religious metaphors, like the metaphors he drew from travel, business, or archeology, were only metaphors. It is admittedly risky to suggest that Freud's energetic and effective similes—Freud's, of all people's!—have no secret messages to convey. After all, Freud consistently and forcefully argued that there are no pure accidents, no uncaused acts, in the mental world, and that one's choice of language, no matter how commonplace, is bound to disclose subterranean meanings to the psychoanalytic investigator. "Sometimes a cigar is just a cigar," that sensible, liberating caution against overinterpretation so often attributed to Freud, seems to have been wished on him by some anonymous phrasemaker. But he might well have said it. Sometimes a cigar *was* just a cigar, even for Freud.

Still, commentators on Freud's thought have been unable to

22. Freud to Silberstein, March 7, 1875. Freud Collection, D2, LC.
23. Freud to Martha Bernays, October 28, 1883. In *Jones* I, 41.
24. Freud to Fliess, February 6, 1899. *Freud-Fliess,* 376 (343).

resist exploiting this loose talk. It is easy to see why. Nothing would more definitively devastate Freud's claim to have originated a branch of science than the discovery that he had merely founded just another doctrinaire sect. It is only too tempting to describe Freud as the pontiff of psychoanalysis, the Committee that his intimates formed around him as the college of cardinals, the fundamental principles informing psychoanalysis as its articles of faith, Freud's disputes with Jung and Adler as heresy trials, and the defectors themselves as apostates. Indeed, Freud's critics have applied these metaphors with barely suppressed smiles of triumph. Let a few instances stand for literally scores. "Perhaps Freud," writes one, "was not fearful enough of the deleterious aspects of religion, for psychoanalysis succeeded in becoming for many a surrogate religion."[25] Freud, writes another, "was a devout believer in 'progress' and treated science as man's sole and sufficient source of valid wisdom. And though he disavowed religion, there is a religious zeal in his sense of mission and service to humanity."[26] A third finds the "Freudian religion" to be a modern phenomenon: "Everyone who wished to be considered enlightened genuflected to Freud before he could proceed with the business at hand. The psychoanalysts became in large measure the 'high priests' of this new religion."[27] In his book *Freud and Religious Belief*, the English social psychologist H. C. Philp recalls an aphorism by

25. Paul Roazen, *Erik H. Erikson: The Power and Limits of a Vision* (1976), 183.
26. Albert C. Outler, *Psychotherapy and the Christian Message* (1954), 43.
27. Camilla M. Anderson, *Beyond Freud: A Creative Approach to Mental Health* (1958), 262–63.

the nineteenth-century French writer Alphonse Karr, "Unbelief is a belief, a very demanding religion," and appropriates the observation to his own purposes: "Science became Freud's faith," is Philp's gloss, "psychoanalysis his sect. Whatever illusions other men might or might not possess, his illusion was science."[28] These are obvious and, as we have seen, virtually irresistible remarks. After all, even Freud's good friend Oskar Pfister found it possible to charge Freud quite directly with being a devotee of a "substitute religion."[29]

But the reasoning that underlies the equation of psychoanalysis with a religion rests on psychological and sociological assumptions that only appear to be self-evident. "It must be admitted," Henry L. Roberts, a distinguished student of Soviet Communism, wrote some years ago, "that a 'secular religion' is not an altogether obvious entity."[30] Precisely. Belief is not a single type of mental act: the grounds, the logic, the tenacity of one belief will differ markedly from those of others. The belief that God exists and the belief that the unconscious exists

28. Philp, *Freud and Religious Belief* (1956), 129.

29. Not even Ernest Jones could resist this game, but at least he restricts Freud's presumed religiosity to his adolescence: Freud's ideal, he writes, was "that of a scientific integrity combined with a wholehearted faith in its ethical value. The word faith is used advisedly, since the analogy between this attitude and that of religious or political ideals is not altogether remote. Like most adolescents Freud had the need to 'believe in something' and in his case the something was Science with a capital." *Jones* I, 40. In 1910, Jones reported to Freud that he had had some trouble getting his "pupil" Bernard Hart, whose publications Freud appreciated, "to take up your work. Ultimately he said, 'Freudism is strictly speaking a religion; you can't *prove* it, but you have to accept it because it works.'" Jones to Freud, March 30, 1910. By permission of Sigmund Freud Copyrights, Wivenhoe.

30. Roberts, *Russia and America: Dangers and Prospects* (1956), 19.

are not, whatever captious critics might say, identical kinds of assertions; they call on quite different evidence and produce quite different results. Still, the term "belief" has become a favorite victim of metaphors taken literally. It should hardly be necessary to observe that when Gladstone called John Stuart Mill the "saint of rationalism," he did not think of him as a true saint but meant to convey with this epithet the decency of Mill's motives and the pure passion of his reformist will.[31] Again, when Edmund Gosse denounced "the hideous new religion of Science" as a deadly threat to all liberty and diversity, he was voicing a vague, highly rhetorical anxiety rather than taking a firmly analyzed intellectual position on the religious nature of modern science.[32]

Not all this talk was irresponsible. There were philosophers in Freud's lifetime who took the notions of science as a religion, and of religion as a science, quite seriously. The most impressive among these was certainly William James, equally distinguished as philosopher and psychologist. His thought is of particular interest to the student of Freud's atheism, for the two men, unlike as they obviously were in their intellectual styles, had a great deal in common. James was, after all, a celebrated analyst of religion, and from a psychological perspective. His seminal Gifford Lectures, as their title makes

31. Gladstone to W. L. Courtney, December 19, 1888. Quoted in Theodor Gomperz, *Essays und Erinnerungen* (1905), 241.
32. Gosse to Robert Ross, quoted in Evan Charteris, *The Life and Letters of Sir Edmund Gosse* (1931), 313.

plain, concentrate on religious *experience,* and their subtitle, "A Study in Human Nature," leaves no doubt that James was interested chiefly in the stuff of human minds rather than in theological disquisitions or ecclesiastical organization. He and Freud occupied much of the same ground.

Significantly, both James and Freud were willing, even eager, to make themselves at home in the shadowy and perilous border regions where science and superstition meet. "Why do so few 'scientists' even look at the evidence for telepathy, so-called?" James asked in his famous essay "The Will to Believe."[33] That was in 1896. Two decades or more later, Freud, the professional skeptic, would be one of the few scientists of mind to take that very risk.[34] The affinities between the two men did not end there. Like Freud, James took his witnesses to faith seriously, was open to the depositions of cranks, fanatics, and visionaries, used his own experience as testimony; he, too, gloried in the astonishing, inexhaustible variety of human experience while he was, at the same time, intent on reducing it to order.

33. James, "The Will to Believe" (1896), in *The Will to Believe,* 10.

34. The comments of Anna Freud, with whom Freud performed some telepathic experiments, are pertinent here if perhaps slightly too uncritical: In hunting for mushrooms, father and daughter "acted out" certain "superstitions." All of it "was such nonsense but such good fun at the time. . . . I believe what interested him in superstitious attitudes was no more than finding the remnants of it in even highly rational people and making fun of it." Telepathy, "thought transference," was something else: "There, I believe, he was trying to be 'fair,' i.e., not treat it as other people had treated psychoanalysis. I never could see that he himself believed in more than the possibility of two unconscious minds communicating with each other without the help of a conscious bridge." She concluded that "the subject must have fascinated, as well as repelled him." Anna Freud to Ernest Jones, November 24, 1955. Archives, British Psycho-Analytical Society, London.

Indeed, for one dazzling moment it even seems as though James and Freud agreed in their diagnosis of what religion is really all about: for Freud, it is the helplessness of the child that stands as the root cause for all the elaborate theological machinery humanity has devised through the ages. James, for his part, exclaims in the middle of his lectures on the varieties of religious experience: "Here is the real core of the religious problem: Help! Help!"[35]

In view of these far from negligible affinities, the differences between Freud and James are all the more instructive. "'Science' in many minds is *genuinely* taking the place of a religion," James wrote, as if to dissent with the greatest possible emphasis from the secular mentality that Freud represents in all its purity. "Where this is so, the scientist treats the laws of nature as objective facts to be *revered*."[36] The italics are mine, the emphasis is James's own. With the dismissive air he assumed when he was arguing with impassioned followers of science, James detected in them a concealed, unworthy, reductionist religiosity: "Certain of our positivists keep chiming to us, that, amid the wreck of every other god and idol, one divinity still stands upright,—that his name is Scientific Truth," and that he commands his followers not to be Theists. "These most conscientious gentlemen think they have jumped off their own feet," emancipating themselves from the shackles of their "subjective propensities." But "they are deluded." What they have done has been to choose among these propensities to "con-

35. William James, *The Varieties of Religious Experience: A Study in Human Nature* (1902), 162.
36. Ibid., 57.

struct, out of the materials given, the leanest, lowest, aridest result,—namely, the bare molecular world,—and they have sacrificed all the rest."[37] Darwinism in particular, James thought, had laid the groundwork "for a new sort of religion of Nature, which has entirely displaced Christianity from the thought of a large part of our generation."[38] Freud, who was second to none in his admiration for Darwin, would have acknowledged his impact on Freud himself and his generation but rejected the accusation that the scientific attitude is a form of reverence, and reductionist reverence at that.

James was, in the teeth of science, a religious man: nothing divine was alien to him. The divinity he carpentered for himself was like no other, a highly individual creation, in need of human aid. "We and God," he concluded, "have business with each other," and he wondered out loud: "Who knows whether the faithfulness of individuals here below to their own poor over-beliefs may not actually help God in turn to be more effectively faithful to his own greater tasks?"[39] In his pragmatist's universe, everyone, including the Deity itself, had to work to make things happen. Impressed as he was with James, Freud, had he read those lines, would have adduced them as just one more proof that philosophers really have nothing useful, even intelligible, to say.

Respecting religious experience as not merely interesting but in essence valid, as the bearer of the deepest truths, James was predictably impatient with the self-confidence of modern sci-

37. James, "Reflex Action and Theism," *The Will to Believe,* 131.
38. *Varieties of Religious Experience,* 91.
39. Ibid., 516–17, 519.

entists. They were making "premature" claims to a monopoly on knowledge. "The universe," he objected, is "a more many-sided affair than any sect, even the scientific sect, allows for."[40] The arrogance of those he chose to call "medical materialists" irritated him; they are, he wrote with his customary vehemence, "only so many belated dogmatists."[41] He did not deny science its share in making important discoveries about human nature; James was not a brilliant psychologist for nothing. His set pieces in *The Varieties of Religious Experience* on Whitman and St. Teresa, two confessors who engaged his interest but not his wholehearted admiration, are splendid exercises of James's scientific imagination. So are his excursions into the analysis of pathological depression masquerading as religious melancholy and his developmental history of inner conflicts.[42] He could grow positively lyrical contemplating the triumphant successes of which modern science could rightfully boast: "When one turns to the magnificent edifice of the physical sciences, and sees how it was reared; what thousands of disinterested moral lives of men lie buried in its mere foundations; what patience and postponement, what choking down of preference, what submission to the icy laws of outer fact are wrought into its very stones and mortar; how absolutely impersonal it stands in its vast augustness,—then how besotted and contemptible seems every little sentimentalist who comes blowing his voluntary smoke-wreaths, and pretending to decide things from out of his private dream!" For James, the school

40. Ibid., 122.
41. Ibid., 19.
42. See ibid., 84–86, 346–48.

of science was "rugged and manly"—he had no higher praise in his vocabulary.[43] But this heartfelt tribute to science did not keep him from disputing its claim to be the sole avenue to truth. Science and religion, James insists, "are both of them genuine keys for unlocking the world's treasure house."[44]

James's attempt to put science in its place was not designed to put it out of court. He envisioned each of humanity's great attempts to know as sovereign in its own sphere. Yet if they were separate, they were not equal. Granted, "physical science" is one of the "good things" the "rationalistic system" has produced. But, having given, James quickly takes away: "Nevertheless, if we look on man's whole mental life as it exists, on the life of men that lies in them apart from their learning and science, and that they inwardly and privately follow, we have to confess that the part of it which rationalism can give and account for is relatively superficial."[45] James never ceased to protest against this incurable superficiality of science. "Instinct leads," he noted in one of his memorable epigrams, "intelligence does but follow."[46] Freud, we know, devoted the best hours of his life to the power of impulse and unreason, but as a devotee of his god logos, he would have regarded James's proposition as sheer blasphemy.

James, though, was inexorable; he saw the tendency to vulgar reductionism and Whiggish optimism as the distinctive mark of materialistic thought. In some prescient paragraphs, written

43. James, "The Will to Believe," *The Will to Believe,* 7.
44. *Varieties of Religious Experience,* 122.
45. Ibid., 73.
46. Ibid., 74.

as though he had Freud's papers on sexuality at his elbow and
was intent on refuting them, James strenuously deplored the
"re-interpretation of religion as perverted sexuality."[47] He deplored no less his many contemporaries, "'scientists' or 'positivists' they are fond of calling themselves—who will tell you
that religious thought is a mere survival, an atavistic reversion
to a type of consciousness which humanity in its more enlightened examples have long since left behind and outgrown."[48] It
is a measure of James's generosity of spirit that even though
he thought Freud a "man obsessed" and bigoted in his incom-
prehension of religion, he could still wish him well. Freud,
after all, was saying precisely such scientific, positivist things
about religion as those James found so deplorable.[49]

Yet James always returned to the recognition that even if
science is inferior to, narrower than, religion, it has much to
contribute to the study of religious phenomena. He found
grounds for cheer in the "impartial classifications and compar-
isons" that had recently "become possible, alongside of the
denunciations and anathemas by which the commerce between
creeds used exclusively to be carried on." He noted with pleasure that "we have the beginnings of a 'Science of Religions,'
so-called," and he modestly hoped that his lectures on their
varieties might be "accounted a crumb-like contribution to
such a science."[50] He noted, too, that philosophy, once it aban-

47. Ibid., 11*n*.
48. Ibid., 118.
49. See William James to Théodore Flournoy, September 28, 1909.
Henry James, ed., *The Letters of William James,* 2 vols. (1920), II, 327–28.
50. *Varieties of Religious Experience,* 433.

doned "metaphysics and deduction for criticism and induction," would become enormously useful, as it transformed itself "from theology into science of religions."[51] Freud could not have said it any better. But Freud was not prepared to believe that this young, flourishing science of religions could ever put an end to the long conflict between the two warring camps. At best, it would put an end to religion.

It is worth repeating that the peace James envisioned did not amount to a merger. "The pivot round which the religious life . . . revolves is the interest of the individual in his private personal destiny." Science, in contrast, "has ended by utterly repudiating the personal point of view. She catalogues her elements and records her laws indifferent as to what purpose may be shown forth by them, and constructs her theories quite careless of their bearing on human anxieties and fates."[52] Freud would have agreed that science constructs its laws indifferent to human wishes. That is, indeed, its very hallmark: it may originate in wishes, but they do not determine its results. At the same time, while Freud, working to establish the theories of psychoanalysis, subsumed the symptoms of each analysand under general rules, he did not permit this pressure for generalization to engross his attention. His unsurpassed case histories are tributes to the fertile interaction of individual with universal in his theory and his practice.

James was uneasily aware that he was swimming against the mainstream of informed thinking in his time, and he acknowledged that even a devout scientist will find his science to be

51. Ibid., 455.
52. Ibid., 491.

atheistic: "Though the scientist may individually nourish a religion, and be a theist in his irresponsible hours, the days are over when it could be said that for Science herself the heavens declare the glory of God and the firmament showeth his handiwork."[53] He conceded that the natural theology pointing to God's work rather than to his words as grounds for belief and adoration, that moderate, sensible faith which had been so comfortable for rationalist Christians for two centuries and more, had come to seem outmoded, naive, almost ludicrous.

James the psychologist and James the philosopher, in short, were at odds with each other. On the one hand, James recognized that science is bound to be irreverent. On the other hand, he was persuaded that reverence is necessary as a ladder to the most exalted truths. In the end, James's fascination with, and commitment to, religious experience gained the upper hand. It is one thing, he thought, and a good thing, to classify; it is better to recognize the modest scope of such an antiseptic activity: "Most cases," he said explicitly, "are mixed cases, and we should not treat our classifications with too much respect."[54] Indeed, with evident pleasure, James subverted his own much-quoted schemes of classification. In the light of the vertiginous diversity of human experience, "the contrast between the healthy and the morbid mind, and between the once-born and the twice-born types . . . cease to be the radical antagonisms which many think them."[55] What truly matters is that "Religion, occupying herself with personal destinies and

53. Ibid.
54. Ibid., 148.
55. Ibid., 488n.

keeping them in contact with the only absolute realities which
we know, must necessarily play an eternal part in human history."[56] In the end, men must move beyond, which is to say,
above, science. For science, he concludes, deals "only with the
symbols of reality" rather than with reality itself.[57] "Humbug
is humbug, even though it bear the scientific name, and the
total expression of human experience, as I view it objectively,
invincibly urges me beyond the narrow 'scientific' bounds. As-
suredly, the real world is of a different temperament—more
intimately built than physical science allows."[58] Freud, too,
was tracking down elusive mysteries, but he thought them in
need of scientific investigation rather than worshipful regard.
James was distinctly not of Freud's persuasion. A little desperately, he resolved the conflict between his regard for science
and his urge toward faith by placing his bets on the will to
believe.

W ith their robust prose, honest self-exploration, psychological penetration, and trusting surrender to higher powers,
William James's writings on religion form a backdrop against
which Freud's unbelief stands out sharply. It is impossible to
conjecture what kind of psychology James would have developed if he had been an atheist like Freud, but it is certain—
and I am devoting the rest of this book to demonstrating this

56. Ibid., 503.
57. Ibid., 498.
58. Ibid., 519.

argument—that if Freud had been a believer like James, he would not have developed psychoanalysis.

Freud was alert to the possibility that he, the self-styled destroyer of illusions, might well be harboring the illusion that he had got beyond them. After sketching the outlines of a culture that should be able to dispense with the consolations religion has to offer, he stopped short: "But I shall moderate my zeal and concede the possibility that I, too, am chasing after an illusion." After all, it is hard to avoid them, and perhaps his optimistic fantasy, too, was "of an illusory nature."[59] This was a handsome concession to his fallibility, but Freud withdrew it almost as soon as he made it. Having allowed that perhaps he, too, had been beguiled by pleasing fantasies, he firmly drew the distinction that mattered to him. "To one difference," he wrote, "I hold fast: my illusions, apart from the fact that there is no penalty for not sharing them, are not incorrigible, like the religious ones, [and] do not have a delusional character. If experience should show—not to me, but to others after me, who think the same way—that we have been mistaken, then we will renounce our expectations."[60]

Freud's defense goes to the core of the argument I want to make in these chapters. He saw psychoanalysis not as a religion: it is susceptible to the criticism of controlled experience as religions are not—to fresh material from the analyst's self-analysis, from case histories, from clinical reports, even at times from experimentation, and above all from one's own

59. *Zukunft einer Illusion, GW* XIV, 376 / *Future of an Illusion, SE* XXI, 48.
60. Ibid., 376 / 53.

analysands, those great teachers. Freud did not explicitly say so, but it is clear that he thought the scientist who obstinately clings to theories that his own work, or that of his colleagues, has discredited is simply not a good scientist. Since Freud wrote, we have learned a good deal more about the psychology of physicists, biologists—and psychoanalysts. It has become evident that Freud idealized their inner freedom, their readiness to confess error, modify their cherished notions, and abandon untenable positions. What matters, though, is not Freud's surviving nineteenth-century innocence about the ways of scientists with inconvenient discomfirming data, but the essential difference between religion and science on which he takes his stand. However imperfectly realized in his work, the distinction he drew—religious ideas are incorrigible, scientific ideas corrigible—defines Freud's fundamental conviction that there are two wholly incompatible styles of thinking in the world, the theological or metaphysical on the one hand, the scientific on the other, and that no mental gymnastics, no effort of will, can ever reconcile them.

In the end, the conflation of psychoanalysis with religion rests on plausible analogies or parallels. But to discover those is remarkably easy work. There are bound to be convergences between psychoanalysis and religion, whether it be Judaism, Protestantism, Catholicism, or Buddhism. But the same convergences, even more striking, subsist between psychoanalysis and pagan, secular philosophy. In 1910, Freud told a correspondent from Palestine who had sought to assimilate Freud's theory of dreams to Talmudic discussions: "My attention has repeatedly been called to the observations in the Talmud about the problems of dreams. But I must say that the approximation to the understanding of the dream among the ancient Greeks is far more striking."[61] Freud would not be typecast.

Whatever the true parallels between Freud's thought and past ideas, they had to be close. How could they be otherwise? For more than two millennia, humans have found themselves problematic. They have puzzled over their motives and their passions, suspected that there is more to the mind than the ideas so conspicuously lodged in consciousness. Across the centuries, literally thousands of self-aware wise men and women have probed into themselves and into others. Some were rabbis, others priests, philosophers, poets, storytellers, even psychologists. It is well known that Freud more than once voiced his envy of creative writers who, with one bold stroke of their imagination, hit upon psychological truths that he had elicited from his analysands only after untold laborious hours of patient listening. Love, hate, pride, guilt, doubt, shame have been essential raw materials for Plato and Sophocles, Shakespeare and Hobbes, Pascal and Goethe, and, in Freud's own century, for Dostoevsky and William James. The anonymous Jews who made up and elaborated the jokes that Freud liked to tell were in their way psychologists, too.

Parallels, then, may hint at much, but they guarantee nothing. Intellectual historians, especially if they extend their researches to the unconscious grounds of the ideas they are studying, practice a more exacting discipline than many have allowed for. They cannot ignore and must not minimize Freud's

61. Freud to A. Drujanow, a Jewish student of folklore, March 3, 1910. Freud Museum, London.

repeated assertions that he was an atheist, an infidel Jew, all his life—even if they must refuse to take such pronouncements as gospel. All that the parallel hunters have established is that universal human concerns are the business of the theologian quite as much as of the psychoanalyst. It is possible to be devout and a disciple of Freud at the same time. We have all met competent psychoanalysts who fast on Yom Kippur. But what this tells us about Freud's cast of mind and the making of psychoanalysis is anything but obvious.

❀ ONE

The Last Philosophe:

"Our God Logos"

In 1918, in a much-quoted letter to his Swiss friend Oskar Pfister, professional pastor and lay analyst, Sigmund Freud asked: "Quite by the way, why did none of the devout create psychoanalysis? Why did one have to wait for a completely godless Jew?"[1] I want in this book to translate these two light-hearted rhetorical questions into three propositions: it was as an atheist that Freud developed psychoanalysis; it was from his atheist vantage point that he could dismiss as well-meaning but futile gestures all attempts to find common ground between faith and unbelief; it was, finally, as a particular kind of atheist, a Jewish atheist, that he was enabled to make his momentous discoveries. Would all believers have been incapacitated on principle from discovering psychoanalysis? Did the first psychoanalyst have to be a godless Jew? Freud asked and did not stay for an answer. His evasion defines my assignment.

I bring no news when I report that Freud was a militant atheist. True, in his early student days at the University of

1. Freud to Pfister, October 9, 1918. *Freud-Pfister,* 64 (63).

Vienna, he toyed with the temptations of theism. He had stumbled into the refreshing and seductive ambience of the philosopher Franz Brentano, an ex-priest who believed in God and respected Darwin at the same time. Freud esteemed him a "damned clever fellow," in fact a genius.[2] But his flirtation with philosophical theology was fleeting and, as his letters attest, really out of character. He was at heart, he told his school friend Eduard Silberstein, a "godless medical man and an empiricist."[3] In 1875, when Brentano's influence on him was at its height, he "temporarily" thought himself "no longer a materialist, also not yet a theist." But he protested that he would sell his godlessness at a high price: "I have no intention of surrendering so quickly and so completely."[4] Nor did he. Rather, measuring himself against that "sharp dialectician," Brentano, he tested the strength of his unbelief—to his satisfaction.[5] Once he had worked his way through the barrage of plausible arguments with which Brentano had overwhelmed him, Freud returned to his atheism and remained there the rest of his days. "Neither in my private life nor in my writings," he wrote a year before he died, "have I ever made a secret of being an out-and-out unbeliever."[6]

All this certainly is not news. Freud, we know, did not keep it a secret. His rivals among psychologists, notably Carl Jung and Alfred Adler, freely remarked on Freud's irreligion as they

2. Freud to Silberstein, March 5, 1875. Freud Collection, D2, LC.
3. Freud to Silberstein, November 8, 1874. Ibid.
4. Freud to Silberstein, March 13–15, 1875. Ibid.
5. Freud to Silberstein, March 27, 1875. Ibid.
6. Freud to Charles Singer, October 31, 1938. *Briefe,* 469.

worked to construct world views of their own. Commentators on Freud's thought from Martin Buber and Erich Fromm to Marthe Robert and Hans Küng have critically canvassed that irreligion, sometimes in exhaustive detail. So have publicists, historians of ideas, and, most of all, theologians. For well over half a century, men of God have shown themselves as fascinated by Freud's aggressive atheism as a subject is by his hypnotist: the ominous figure of Freud, the godless Jew, will not leave them alone.

Only disciples of Marx have found Freud not materialistic enough or, worse, the wrong kind of materialist. Mikhail Bakhtin, one of a handful among Marxist theoreticians who took Freud seriously, concluded that "Freudianism" was "a doctrine profoundly, organically alien to Marxism"—an observation that Freud would have greeted with relief and pleasure. In contrast, he would doubtless have objected strongly to Bakhtin's conclusion that his theory amounted to "a SPIRITUAL MONISM."[7] For his part Karl Kautsky, whom insiders nicknamed "the pope of German Marxism," poured scorn on what he derided as Freud's obscene pansexualism: "When one reads Freud, one could think all of man is nothing but an appendage to his sexual organs." But in the end, Kautsky found Freud not really a materialist at all, not even a dirty old one: "Freudian psychoanalysis in medical practice seems to me fundamen-

7. "V. N. Volochinov," *Le Freudisme* (1927; tr. Guy Verret, 1980), 191, 195. This book is one of Bakhtin's "disputed texts"; there is a high probability, though no certainty, that Bakhtin wrote most if not all of this book, hiding behind Volochinov's name. See Katerina Clark and Michael Holquist, *Mikhail Bakhtin* (1984), 146–47, 160–65, 171–85.

tally nothing other than the transfer of some techniques of the Catholic confessional into the physician's consulting room."[8]

The religious, though, including those who went to confession, found Freud unspiritual enough. A scholarly survey of 1970 summarizing the Roman Catholic indictment of Freud's subversive thought lists no fewer than fourteen counts: materialism, naturalism, skepticism, mechanism, evolutionism, rationalism, empiricism, to say nothing of positivism, relativism, physiologism, biologism, psychologism, historicism, and, of course, atheism.[9] To be sure, some of these resounding reproaches are imprecise in the extreme: one man's materialism is another man's idealism. Others are mutually contradictory: it is hard to be found guilty of physiologism and psychologism at the same time. But the general drift of these charges is accurate enough. They point to Freud's explicit and extreme conviction that religious belief is a kind of cultural neurosis: a survival of childish helplessness into adult life, a supreme instance of wishful thinking, an illusion hovering perilously close to delusional madness.[10] I need not demonstrate that Freud was

8. Kautsky, *Die materialistische Geschichtsauffassung,* 2 vols. (1927), I, 219, 340.

9. See Kasimir Birk, *Sigmund Freud und die Religion* (1970), 114–15.

10. It is interesting to see Freud's scientific, wholly "disenchanted" view of religion at work in his case histories. In the most famous of his case reports, the case of the Wolf-Man, Freud analyzed his patient's childhood transformation from a sadistic and phobic little boy to an obsessively pious one as the result of his mother's religious teachings and his introduction to the Bible stories. With his patient, Freud suavely notes, religion managed to accomplish the purposes for which it is usually introduced into the educational process: it helped him to sublimate his urgent sexual impulses and gave him a feeling of community with all of mankind. This process socialized him, made him into a good boy who was receptive to being educated. "From

an atheist before he became a psychoanalyst.[11] What I want to demonstrate, rather, is that Freud became a psychoanalyst in large part *because* he was an atheist.

Freud was a loyal son of the Enlightenment, the last of the philosophes. Pfister saw this clearly, if a little tendentiously: "Your substitute religion," he informed Freud bluntly, "is in essence the Enlightenment thought of the eighteenth century in proud, fresh modern guise."[12] Freud, though he did not think of his science as a substitute religion, was happy to claim the Enlightenment as his intellectual ancestor. It is significant that he should choose to disclaim any originality for his critique of religion precisely in *The Future of an Illusion,* his most sustained assault. He recognized, and drew strength from, his dependence on enlightened minds of the past: "I have said nothing that other, better men have not said before me far more completely, forcibly, and impressively. The names of these men are well known; I shall not cite them: the impression

---

the History of an Infantile Neurosis" (1918), *SE* XVII, 1–122, esp. 62–68, 114–17. The Rat Man, too, underwent a religious phase which Freud analyzed with quite as much distance as that of the Wolf-Man. (See "Notes upon a Case of Obsessional Neurosis" [1909], *SE* X, 153–318, esp. 169–70, 301–02.) The great French neurologist Jean-Martin Charcot, with whom Freud studied in Paris in the winter of 1885, put his studies into the service of anticlericalism: he was firmly convinced that many religious manifestations can be reduced to pure hysteria. Havelock Ellis offered much evidence to the same effect.

11. Hans Küng makes this point in *Freud and the Problem of God* (tr. Edward Quinn, 1979), 75.

12. Pfister to Freud, November 24, 1927. *Freud-Pfister,* 123 (115).

should not be awakened that I want to place myself in their
ranks."[13] We may supply these names: Voltaire, Diderot, Feuerbach, Darwin.

As this succinct list indicates, Freud the cultivated Central
European absorbed the Enlightenment in large part directly:
he had a good deal of the French, even more of the German,
Enlightenment at his disposal. He could quote Voltaire and
Diderot, Lichtenberg and Lessing, with ease. Their writings
provided him with an intellectual base and with telling, quot-
able passages. But beyond them, Freud lived in an atmosphere
of what William James called "medical materialism." The scientific positivists who were Freud's teachers at medical school
and beyond—the physiologist Ernst Brücke, the brain anatomist Theodor Meynert, and the internist Hermann Nothnagel,
all equally eminent—had taken the program of the Enlightenment into the chemist's laboratory and the anatomist's au-
ditorium. Together all these influences, subtly interwoven and
mutually reinforcing, made up Freud's mental universe, a universe from which he drew not so much the concrete propositions
as the essential attitudes underlying psychoanalysis.

To be sure, Freud did claim originality for his work. Without that it would scarcely have deserved the world's, or the
historian's, attention. "I have merely—this is the only thing
new in my exposition—added to the critique of my great predecessors some psychological grounds."[14] But it was as the last
of the philosophes that Freud denigrated the religious way—

13. *Die Zukunft einer Illusion* (1927), *GW* XIV, 358 / *The Future of an
Illusion*, SE XXI, 35.
14. Ibid.

oscure. The researcher holds literally nothing sac-
e recognizes no boundaries to his systematic
o exemption from his voyeur's privilege. Nothing is
or too low, for science. As early as the seventeenth
pinoza, one of the two or three philosophers Freud
ssed to admire, had laid it down that one must read
as one reads all other books: critically. The philo-
ound this rule of reading eminently congenial. It was
n character for them to select holy writ and other re-
texts as favorite targets for disrespectful analysis, pre-
because these texts had escaped such scrutiny for
es. The philosophes took pride in their mission: like so
modern heirs of Lucretius, they made it their assignment
aken the world from the enchantment in which magicians
priests had held it imprisoned since pagan antiquity.
he vanguard in this assault on credulity were the Deists
he late seventeenth and early eighteenth centuries. With
ost indecent glee, they uncovered evidence for the barbar-
s, the contradictions, the absurdities in the Book that had
long served as the final, indisputable, inspired authority to
eologians and literate laymen alike. They questioned the au-
henticity of the Gospels, exposed prophecies that had remained unfulfilled, excoriated fanatical monks and persecuting
clerics, ridiculed theological reasoning, ventured to doubt the
veracity of miracles and the divinity, the very historical existence, of Christ. Freud carried on their work with his own
corrosive intellectual device, the psychoanalytic method. "I do
not know," he wrote to Pfister in 1928, "whether you have
guessed the secret tie between my [book on] lay analysis and

any religious way—of understanding the world as wholly incompatible with the scientific way. This distinction was, if I
may use the word, sacred to him; he thought the incompati-
bility of science and religion absolutely fundamental and completely incurable. The philosophes of the early generation, those
born in the late seventeenth century, could still muster some
wry sympathy for the theological eccentricities of thinkers they
admired: Voltaire described Newton's obsessive researches into
biblical chronology with a kind of amused benevolence.[15] But
he was confident that Newton, to his mind the greatest man
who ever lived, had made his earthshaking discoveries in spite
of his incursions into scholastic pedantry and esoteric superstition rather than because of them. Such a genial allowance for
the vagaries of splendid minds was an exercise in the historical
imagination. It could not obscure the philosophes' detestation
of what they disparaged as the credulous cast of mind, that
religion-ridden way of explaining man and nature they thought
so fatally inferior to the critical spirit, the spirit they professed
and in part practiced. It would be the detestation rather than
the sympathy that Freud made his own.

Freud appropriated the whole range of the Enlightenment's
agenda, its ideals and its methods, its very language. His debt
to secular eighteenth-century thought extends even to details
of political tactics: in the spirit of the philosophes, Freud at
times advocated an Aesopian self-censorship in setting forth
his subversive ideas. The men of the Enlightenment had appreciated, and vigorously debated, the need for prudence in

15. See above all Voltaire, *Lettres philosophiques sur les Anglais* (1734), esp.
letters XIV and XVII.

two directions: prudence in face of arbitrary, often vindictive government censors intent on stamping out impiety, and prudence in face of the uncultivated populace who, once their superstitious fear of a vengeful God had been lifted, were likely to sink into a life of dissipation and crime. A century and a half later, Freud wondered about precisely the same sorts of risk. Unlike the philosophes, to whom evasiveness and subterfuges became second nature, Freud deprecated any deviation from candor. But in the tense political atmosphere of the mid-1930s, he held back his antireligious papers on Moses and monotheism lest the powerful Roman Catholic hierarchy have psychoanalysis banned in Austria.

Freud even worried, in true eighteenth-century fashion, about the more general consequences of publishing the full truth about religion. The scientific spirit which scorns all supernatural faith, he thought, poses no danger for "the educated and for intellectual workers." With them, the "substitution of religious motives" by "other, worldly ones" would "proceed noiselessly." But "the great mass of the uneducated, the oppressed, who have every reason to be enemies of culture," were another matter. "As long as they do not learn that one no longer believes in God, all is well." For, once they do learn it, will they not feel free to kill their neighbors? It was, Freud conceded, a problem.[16] Acting like a latter-day Voltaire, he went so far as to counsel his followers to caution. "I have heard," he wrote to Ernest Jones in the spring of 1921, "of some danger to be expected from reprinting in English your

16. *Zukunft einer Illusion,* GW XIV, 362–63 / *Future of an Illusion,* SE XXI, 39.

blasphemous paper
lished this long ess
my sympathies go,"
be foolish to provoke
gland as long as our
remarkable island."[17]

These are matters of
weightier evidence proving
of the philosophes: his ins
world view—*Weltanschauung*-
of mind that define the ment
reflected this sovereignty of the
he wrote in his great program
"Everything must be examined,
up, without exception and withou
iterated this view in his article or
"Facts may be distributed among
divinity, the phenomena of nature,
The first belong to theology, the secon
last to history properly speaking. All
criticism."[19] The secular animus of enli
in its wake, of Freud's thought dominates
nouncements.

Their meaning for the philosophes, and

17. Freud to Jones, April 6, 1921, in English. Fr
LC.
18. "Encyclopédie," in Diderot's *Encyclopédie. Oeuvres*
Assézat and Maurice Tourneux, 20 vols. (1875–77), XIV,
19. "Fait," ibid., XV, 3.

thing but o
rosanct. H
curiosity,
too high,
century, S
ever profe
the Bibl
sophes f
wholly
ligious
cisely
centur
many
to aw
and
T
of
al
iti
so
th
t

my [*Future of an*] *Illusion*. In the first I want to protect analysis from the doctors, in the latter from the priests."[20] Freud's assimilation of the procedures and presuppositions of psycho-analysis to those of science was nothing if not truculent.

The cardinal text in which Freud explores this point of view is his paper on a Weltanschauung, the last among his *New Introductory Lectures on Psychoanalysis,* written from the ripe, late perspective of his mid-seventies. Its English editor, James Strachey, thought it "only indirectly related to psychoanaly-sis."[21] But that is an unduly narrow definition of Freud's en-terprise. The paper is a declaration of principle, a kind of metapsychoanalysis. Its placement at the end of what Freud intended as his most comprehensive exposition of his ideas is strategic, not fortuitous. Psychoanalysis, Freud insists, has a right to a passport valid everywhere. This claim functions as the researcher's counterpart to what psychoanalysts call the fundamental rule of their therapy: the patient must free himself to say everything, absolutely everything, that comes to his mind, no matter how boring, trivial, irrelevant, scurrilous, or obscene it may appear to him. The fundamental rule governing Freud's creation is no less sweeping: psychoanalysis is "a spe-cialized science, a branch of psychology—depth psychology or psychology of the unconscious" which, "quite unsuited to form a world view of its own, must accept that of science." As such, "it asserts that there is no source for knowing the world other than the intellectual working over of observations carefully re-

20. Freud to Pfister, November 25, 1928. *Freud-Pfister,* 136 (126).
21. "Editor's Note" to *New Introductory Lectures in Psycho-Analysis* (1932), *SE,* XXII, 4.

viewed." This is the point: *there is no other source.* Freud explicitly rejects such glittering but, to his mind, spurious alternatives as "revelation, intuition, or divination."[22] "There is," as he put it tersely in *The Future of an Illusion,* "no court of appeal higher than reason."[23]

Anticipating his critics in his best forensic manner, Freud acknowledged that what they liked to call his scientism was open to objections. Some thought it unfeeling or cheerless— William James for one found all naturalistic world views sad. But Freud, without mentioning James's name, energetically rejected such cavils. Far from neglecting the needs of the mind, psychoanalysis makes those very needs into objects of scientific research. Psychoanalysis, in fact, may take pride in its role of active spokesman rather than passive beneficiary of the scientific spirit: "Its contribution to science consists precisely in the extension of research into the mental field." One might say that "without such a psychology, science would be very incomplete."[24]

This self-assured posture enables Freud to meet another grave objection. People like to think that when they assign science one domain and philosophy another, they are being "civilized, tolerant, broad-minded, free of petty prejudices." But this cos-

22. "Über eine Weltanschauung," *Neue Folge der Vorlesungen, GW,* XV, 171 / "Question of a Weltanschauung," *New Introductory Lectures, SE* XXII, 158.

23. *Zukunft einer Illusion, GW* XIV, 350 / *Future of an Illusion, SE* XXI, 28.

24. "Über eine Weltanschauung," *Neue Folge der Vorlesungen, GW* XV, 171 / "Question of a Weltanschauung," *New Introductory Lectures, SE* XXII, 159.

mopolitan evenhandedness is nothing better than an abject surrender to unscientific modes of thought: "The truth cannot be tolerant, it admits no compromises and reservations."[25] Voltaire had anticipated this rebuttal by almost two centuries. Confronted with the charge that his famous battle cry, *Écrasez l'infâme,* was merely destructive, he replied that there are times when one must destroy before one can build.[26] The critical spirit can do its constructive work only after it has liberated mankind from the shackles of belief. Voltaire gladly admitted that he and his associates were being intolerant, but it was an intolerance directed only against intolerance. This was the sort of intolerance that Freud welcomed and applied. "Research," he wrote, "regards all domains of human activity as its own and must become pitilessly critical when another power wants to confiscate a part of it for itself."[27] Subtle reasoners might want to retain some authority for metaphysics or theology by postulating several types of truth to which they have privileged access. But Freud provocatively adopted the naive standpoint of the common man: there is only one truth.[28] An idea may be lovely or consoling, but to leap from that to the assertion that the idea is therefore true only cripples the intellect. "Religion," Diderot had written in 1759, "retreats to the extent

25. Ibid., 171–72 / 160.
26. See Peter Gay, *Voltaire's Politics: The Poet as Realist* (1959), passim, esp. ch. 5.
27. "Über eine Weltanschauung," *Neue Folge der Vorlesungen, GW* XV, 172–73 / "Question of a Weltanschauung," *New Introductory Lectures, SE* XXII, 160.
28. This deliberate, almost ostentatious intellectual populism resembles his acceptance of the popular notion, much favored by the uneducated, that dreams have meanings and can be interpreted.

that philosophy advances."[29] Freud agreed: men of good will could erect the house of science only on the ruins of religion. "Of the three powers"—art, philosophy, religion—"that may contest the very soil of science," he wrote, "religion alone is the serious enemy."[30]

Freud, then, saw science as ringed by rivals, and this perception, too, placed him squarely into the camp of the Enlightenment. He was not afraid of art: it is essentially benevolent and harmless. Philosophy is a rather more troublesome competitor. In itself, Freud suggested, it "is not opposed to science; it acts like a science, works in part with the same methods, but departs from it by clinging to the illusion of being able to deliver a seamless and coherent picture of the world." It sustains this illusion by exaggerating the knowledge it can glean from logical operations or from sheer intuition. But, then, like art, philosophy can do little harm. After all, it "has no direct influence on the great mass of men," confined as it is to "a small number even among the thin top layer of intellectuals." In ominous contrast, "religion is a prodigious power disposing over mankind's strongest emotions."[31]

Two centuries earlier, the Enlightenment had taken much the same position, in the same gladiatorial spirit. Pugnacious

29. Diderot to Sophie Volland (October 30, 1759). *Correspondance*, ed. Georges Roth, 16 vols. (1955–70), II, 297.

30. "Über eine Weltanschauung," *Neue Folge der Vorlesungen*, *GW* XV, 173 / "Question of a Weltanschauung," *New Introductory Lectures*, *SE* XXII, 160.

31. Ibid.

participants in a great debate over the nature of mind and world and God, the philosophes often acted as great simplifiers. They visualized themselves as the forces of light arrayed against the forces of darkness—the church, any church—and against supernatural belief, no matter how moderate. Yet their reading in the history of philosophy compelled them to complicate this melodramatic vision: they assigned a special place to the ambitious metaphysical systems that Descartes and Hobbes, Spinoza and Malebranche and Leibniz, had devised in the seventeenth century. Had they possessed Freud's technical vocabulary, the philosophes would doubtless have characterized these systems as symptoms of the fancied omnipotence of thought. Metaphysics appeared to the philosophes as a kind of unworldly rationalism attesting to humanity's impressive gift for verbal virtuosity and sophisticated self-deception. Descartes, Malebranche, and the others had left the world as they had found it—no better understood, no better off. It had been the singular merit of the critical spirit that it had traded dazzling acrobatics for solid knowledge.

That is why the Enlightenment prized Francis Bacon, who had so trenchantly exposed the disputes of the philosophers as linguistic games and so effectively pleaded the case for experience. That, too, is why they singled out Newton, in David Hume's encomium, as "the greatest and rarest genius that ever rose for the ornament and instruction of the species."[32] Newton's greatness rested not just on his uncanny genius for penetrating the mysteries of the universe but quite as much on

32. Hume, *History of England* (1754–62; 8 vol. ed. 1780), VIII, 326.

the method he had followed on his lonely voyage of discovery. Had he not said, plainly, that he feigned no hypotheses? Setting aside the epistemological difficulties that this sweeping dictum raises, the philosophes read it as a call to the sort of thinking that made a difference: as a giant leap from the empty *esprit de système* of the seventeenth to the fertile *esprit systématique* of the eighteenth century.[33]

No wonder the century of the Enlightenment was crowded with aspiring Newtons of the mind, or Newtons of society. It seemed that only the critical spirit which had revolutionized the study of the universe could revolutionize the study of mankind. By mid-century, the abbé de Condillac, the most brilliant student of philosophic method and of language the eighteenth century produced, urged his fellows to take their cue from the natural scientists rather than from the metaphysicians: "Today," he wrote in his masterwork, the *Traité des systèmes* of 1749, "a few physical scientists, above all the chemists, are concentrating on collecting phenomena, for they have recognized that one must possess the effects of nature, and discover their mutual dependence, before one poses principles that explain them. The example of their predecessors has been a good lesson to them; they at least wish to avoid the errors that the mania for systems has brought in its train. If only all the philosophers would imitate them!"[34] The philosophes thought of themselves

33. The most illuminating discussion of this critical distinction remains Ernst Cassirer, *The Philosophy of the Enlightenment* (1932; tr. Fritz C. A. Koelln and James P. Pettegrove, 1951), ch. 1.

34. Condillac, *Traité des systèmes*, in *Oeuvres*, ed. Georges Le Roy, 3 vols. (1947–51), I, 127.

as philosophers, but of a very special order: they liked to see their kind of philosophizing as an approximation to the scientific method. The rest, they were sure, is frivolity: the philosophy in which metaphysicians traded was the superstition of an educated elite, paying homage not to saints or miracles, but to words.

This bold redefinition of true philosophy as criticism, or as scientific method, survived into Freud's century and flourished there. It stands as the most distinctive quality of Ludwig Feuerbach's thought. Among all nineteenth-century philosophers, Feuerbach was probably the philosophes' most indisputable heir. A rebellious and outspoken polemicist, he must have seduced more young readers away from religion than anyone else in his age, not excluding Darwin. "We were all Feuerbachians," Friedrich Engels wrote, recalling the early 1840s.[35] Even those who, like Marx, boasted that they had moved beyond Feuerbach never quite erased their debt to him. For all his later disparagement of philosophy and philosophers, the young Freud stood with Engels and Marx in his appreciation of this Fauve among German nineteenth-century thinkers. "Among all philosophers," he wrote while he was a student at the University of Vienna, "I worship and admire this man the most."[36]

There was a great deal to admire. Intellectually the most robust of the left-wing Hegelians, Feuerbach cultivated a style free from the characteristic abstractions and aridities marring German academic prose, and a pugilistic manner that charmed,

35. See Marx W. Wartofsky, *Feuerbach* (1977), xix.
36. Freud to Silberstein, March 7, 1875. Freud Collection, D2, LC.

or appalled, his readers as he battled against the "silly and perfidious judgments" of his detractors.[37] He was not a Freudian before his time, but he had much to teach Freud: his self-assigned task was to unmask theology so as to uncover its all-too-mundane roots in human experience. Theology must become anthropology. Obsessed with religion, Feuerbach labored to bring it down to earth that he might make a divinity of man. This was not exactly one of Freud's ambitions. But if Feuerbach was not properly speaking an atheist, he was a writer calculated to make atheists. "To be sure," this nineteenth-century Voltaire wrote about *The Essence of Christianity,* his best-known treatise, "my book is negative." Yet he insisted that his adversary was not the "human essence of religion" but its "unhuman side" alone.[38] Theology in all its existing forms had never remotely approached the fundamental truths about religion. Nor had traditional philosophy, which, he thought, was only theology without myths. These truths must be sought in man alone.

In the manner of the philosophes before and of Freud after him, Feuerbach was only marginally less critical of philosophers than of theologians. He "unconditionally" rejected what he derided as "absolute, *immaterial, self-satisfied speculation,*" and proffered his own thinking as the very antithesis, the "dissolution," of such empty exercises.[39] He acknowledged—or,

37. "Vorwort" to the second edition of *Das Wesen des Christenthums* (1841; 2d ed., 1843), iii. (Omitted in the famous translation by George Eliot, first published in 1854.)

38. Ibid., xii.

39. Ibid., ix–xi.

rather, advertised—that he lacked "a certain talent," the talent for the "formal philosophical, the systematic, the encyclopedic-methodological."[40] This did not trouble Feuerbach any more than Freud's urbanely confessed tone-deafness to philosophy would later trouble Freud: Feuerbach was in search of an investigative method that would lead him to reality. Religion, he noted in his famous definition, "is the dream of the human mind," but, he added presciently, "even in dreams we do not find ourselves in Nothingness or in Heaven, but on earth, in the realm of reality," seen "in the enchanting appearance of the imagination and of caprice."[41] In the service of his search for the real, Feuerbach denied his philosophy the name of philosophy and refused the very title of philosopher: "I am nothing but an intellectual researcher into nature—*geistiger Naturforscher.*"[42] The name aptly applies to Freud, who so tenaciously insisted that psychoanalysis can happily shelter under the world view of science, and shelter nowhere else.

Their positive self-identifications as much as their disclaimers, then, authenticate Feuerbach's and Freud's kinship to a clan whose family tree reaches back to the days of Newton and Locke and beyond. The relation of "reason to religion," Feuerbach wrote, "amounts only to the destruction of an *illusion*—an illusion, however, which is by no means insignificant but whose effect on mankind, rather, is utterly pernicious."[43] This

40. Feuerbach to Christian Kapp, November 1840. In Wartofsky, *Feuerbach,* 202.

41. *Wesen des Christenthums,* xv.

42. Ibid., x; and see Wartofsky, *Feuerbach,* 201.

43. *Wesen des Christenthums,* 408.

is precisely what Freud had in mind when he described himself as a "destroyer of illusions" who had "spent a great part" of his life destroying his "own illusions and those of mankind."[44] But in their fundamental appraisal of religion, their differences were far-reaching. What Feuerbach had prized as a reality, the divine in man which conventional theology had obscured, was to Freud's mind just another illusion. Freud was not far off when he told his Swiss friend Ludwig Binswanger in 1925 that while he had read Feuerbach "in young years eagerly and with enjoyment," it seemed to him "that the effect was not a lasting one."[45] But as a young unbeliever, Freud had found Feuerbach a valued resource, a companion on his voyage to freedom from faith.

Freud would have been the first to admit that his indefatigable harassment of that illusion, religion, was anything but disinterested, anything but detached scientific investigation. Immersed as he was in European culture, he wove his commitment to the supremacy of science into the very texture of his intellectual style. But his private experience and his emotional evolution also left their deposits on his campaign. Not

44. Freud to Romain Rolland, recorded in Rolland's *journal intime* under March 4, 1923 (I owe this reference to Dr. David S. Werman; see Werman, "Sigmund Freud and Romain Rolland," *Int. Rev. Psycho-Anal.,* IV [1977], 225–41).

45. Freud to Binswanger, February 22, 1925. By permission of Sigmund Freud Copyrights, Wivenhoe. (Also reprinted in Ludwig Binswanger, *Erinnerungen an Freud* [1956], 90.)

surprisingly, commentators have pounced on these subterranean origins of his atheism. It would have been an astonishing oversight, or a mark of almost superhuman forbearance, if they had failed to turn Freud's analytic instruments against him, failed to trace the roots of his secularism back to unmastered childhood traumas. In his substantial survey of psychoanalysis and religious experience, W. W. Meissner, Jesuit and psychoanalyst, solemnly undertakes to reject reductionism and to meet Freud's arguments on their own grounds. But he cannot resist observing: "It seems clear that Freud's religious views, perhaps more than any other aspect of his work and his psychology, reflect underlying and unresolved ambivalences and conflicts stemming from the earliest psychic strata. Behind the Freudian argument about religion stands Freud the man, and behind Freud the man, with his prejudices, beliefs, and convictions, lurks the shadow of Freud the child."[46] Gregory Zilboorg, a psychoanalyst whose religious odyssey included rejecting his orthodox Jewish heritage, embracing Quakerism, and finally converting to Roman Catholicism, was more specific than Meissner. He thought he had found the origins of Freud's refusal to apply his own insights to his study of religion in an early personal tragedy. When he was three, his cherished Roman Catholic nurse, Freud's first love, who had taken him to churches and taught him the "truths" of religion, was dismissed and sent to prison for some petty thefts. "Freud devoted not only forty years, but a life-time, to trying to undo the

---

46. Meissner, *Psychoanalysis and Religious Experience* (1984), vii.

catastrophe that befell him in his childhood." Inevitably, Zilboorg thought, he failed.[47] Freud's deeply flawed analysis of religion, his shallow "scientism," was the result.

It seems only fair to psychoanalyze the first psychoanalyst; Freud's adoption of his world view, and the fervor with which he defended it, must have been, as they say, in character.[48] His appetite for knowledge, and his impatience with any obstacles in the way of his impassioned researches, went far beyond the ordinary. But the scientific agenda he pursued all his adult life went far beyond its origins. What is more, the instances of wild analysis I have just cited come nowhere near exhausting the complex, diverse situations in which that agenda originated. The very intricacies of his family life—an elderly father, a handsome young mother, half-brothers of his mother's generation, a nephew older than himself—proved spurs to his often bewildered but tirelessly pursued investigations. Freud's need to know amounted, as he confessed, to a kind of "greed."[49]

47. Zilboorg, "Love in Freudian Psychoanalysis" (1953), in Zilboorg, *Psychoanalysis and Religion,* ed. Margaret Stone Zilboorg (1967), 139.

48. Probably the most interesting efforts to apply Freud's methods in the study of Freud's writings are Marie Balmary's aptly titled *Psychoanalyzing Psychoanalysis: Freud and the Hidden Fault of the Father* (1979; tr. Ned Lukacher, 1982) and Marthe Robert's *From Oedipus to Moses: Freud's Jewish Identity* (1974; tr. Ralph Manheim, 1976). The first seeks to explicate Freud's theories via the unfinished business of his relations to his father, an effort to spin out the long consequences of the Oedipus complex through a reading of Freud's repressed inconsistencies and contradictions. The second, more charitable, gives Freud's thought an essentially "familial" reading: Freud is "Oedipus-Freud, Son of Jakob."

49. See "Selbstdarstellung," *GW* XIV, 34 / "Autobiographical Study," *SE* XX, 8.

There was, besides, not just oral neediness in that appetite; it was propelled forward by urgent libidinal pressures. The ideas of Darwin, Freud reports, "attracted" him mightily when he was a young student. And that much-cited lecture on Nature that he heard as a schoolboy and that, he testifies, decided him to study medicine rather than law rhapsodically hailed Nature as a beneficent, nourishing, never exhausted, and never denying mother—a sensual and maternal deity wholly different from the cruel, heedless, destructive Nature he would delineate in his late writings.[50] Still, more than libido was involved in this Freudian passion, more than sublimated childish investigations into the facts of life: in a famous autobiographical passage in his *Interpretation of Dreams,* he confessed that he worked best in an atmosphere of tension and combat, of love and hate. He had always needed, and always managed to provide himself with, a friend and an enemy.[51]

In his scientific work, religion became the principal, the ideal enemy. It is true that for Freud, as for so many other unbelievers, Roman Catholicism occupied a particularly conspicuous place in the catalogue of villains to be overthrown. As Rome was in Freud's unconscious the longed-for city he could not bring himself to visit until he had analyzed away some deep-seated inhibitions, so Rome, too, was headquarters of the mighty adversary whose inexhaustible resources and adroit maneuvers Freud had observed at first hand in Vienna all his life. But the Catholic Church was only the worst in a

50. Ibid.
51. *Traumdeutung, GW* II–III, 487 / *Interpretation of Dreams, SE* V, 483.

bad lot. For Freud all religions were tainted with superstition; all, however rationalistic or unpolitical, were, to repeat, the enemy.

There is still more to the formation of his prosecutorial style than this. It owed much to the eminent professors in whose laboratories he worked in the late 1870s and early 1880s. These were the medical materialists of whom I have spoken. They did not make him into an atheist; they did not awaken his hostility to religion. But they gave him the best possible grounds for both. The catalogue of heroes he liked to compile in those years was a catalogue of scientists. As he told his school friend Silberstein in the late summer of 1875, after an exhilarating summer in England, these heroes included such British natural scientists as John Tyndall, Thomas Huxley, Sir Charles Lyell, Charles Darwin.[52] Freud made no less room in his pantheon for German scientists. Early in 1875, he informed Silberstein that he was planning to spend the winter semester at the University of Berlin, to hear the lectures of Emil Du Bois-Reymond, Hermann Helmholtz, and Rudolf Virchow: "I am looking forward to it like a child."[53] In the end nothing came of Freud's plan; his intellectual allegiances grew more differentiated as he wrestled with Brentano's seductive theism and, after that, gradually departed from his teachers' neurological view of the mind. In the long run the impact on him of Brücke, Nothnagel, Meynert, and their colleagues depended far less on the precise structure of their ideas than on their fundamental

52. Freud to Silberstein, September 9, 1875. Freud Collection, D2, LC.
53. Freud to Silberstein, January 24, 1875. Ibid.

orientation: positivistic, atheistic, deterministic.[54] In 1898, Wilhelm Fliess, then Freud's closest friend, sent Freud the two volumes of Helmholtz's collected lectures as a Christmas present.[55] It is as telling that the gift should have been Helmholtz as that the occasion should have been Christmas.

The man who had doubtless the strongest claim to be Freud's "idol" was Ernst Brücke, that cultivated, demanding, feared, internationally renowned German physiologist under whose supervision Freud worked for more than six happy years, between 1876 and 1882. He called Brücke, flatly, "the greatest authority that worked upon me."[56] Brücke had a wholehearted and articulate aversion to all mysterious explanations drawn from romantic *Naturphilosophie* or, worse, from theology. His celebrated lectures on physiology, which Freud heard before their publication in 1876, were wholly unencumbered by any metaphysical burdens, wholly at home in materialism. All natural phenomena are, Brücke argues, phenomena of motion; he

54. Jones has put it well: Freud's "emancipation from this influence [of Brücke] consisted not in renouncing the principles, but in becoming able to apply them empirically to mental phenomena while dispensing with any anatomical basis. . . . Brücke would have been astonished, to put it mildly, had he known that one of his favorite pupils, one apparently a convert to the strict faith, was later, in his famous wish theory of the mind, to bring back into science the ideas of 'purpose,' 'intention,' and 'aim' which had just been abolished from the universe. We know, however, that when Freud did bring them back he was able to reconcile them with the principles in which he had been brought up; he never abandoned determinism for teleology." *Jones* I, 45.

55. See ibid., I, 292.

56. "Nachwort" to *Die Frage der Laienanalyse* (1927), *GW* XIV, 290 / Postscript to *The Question of Lay Analysis*, *SE* XX, 253.

allowed no room in his thought for occult forces, let alone divine intervention. Brücke's close lifelong friend Emil Du Bois-Reymond took the same view: the natural scientist—*Naturforscher*—he wrote, is not hampered by "theological preconceptions."[57] In the two-volume edition of his lectures, dedicated to Brücke, God does not appear. But the Enlightenment does, in appreciative essays on Diderot and Voltaire.[58] This is the mental world in which Freud made his home and from which psychoanalysis eventually emerged. He found it emotionally congenial and intellectually satisfying. But its outlines had first been drawn in the zestful, aggressive critical writings of the eighteenth-century philosophes.

Zestful as they were, and their reputation to the contrary, the men of the Enlightenment were not facile, shallow optimists.[59] While their high morale, and the bracing triumphs of the natural sciences, at times made them victims of easy hopes, they were keenly aware that to conquer the palpable ignorance of the unlettered and the adroitly concealed ignorance of the learned was the most arduous of assignments. Their disbelief in a vengeful god and in original sin only rarely seduced them into utopian dreams of quick solutions. They knew

57. Du Bois-Reymond, "Über die Grenzen des Naturerkennens" (1872), in *Reden von Emil Du Bois-Reymond*, 2 vols., ed. Estelle Du Bois-Reymond (1885; 2d enlarged ed., 1912), I, 461.

58. See among others, "Voltaire als Naturforscher" (1868) and "Zu Diderots Gedächtnis" (1884), in ibid., I, 318–48, and II, 285–300.

59. See Peter Gay, *The Enlightenment: An Interpretation*, 2 vols. (1966, 1969), passim, esp. II, 98–125.

that vast areas on the map of knowledge, whether in the study of nature, of man, or of society, were still wholly unexplored. They knew, too, that the instruments of inquiry they had at hand, or were devising, were still crude and primitive. They knew, finally, that their incursions into holy ground must inevitably arouse the most obstinate resistance. One cardinal virtue they discovered in their idol, Newton, and valiantly tried to emulate was what they called his philosophical modesty. They read his famous disclaimer, "hypotheses non fingo," as a warning against excessive expectations no less than as an injunction to give experience primacy. Turgot spoke for the enlightened consensus when he praised "the simplicity, the prudent circumspection" of Newton's thought.[60] If, by the mid–eighteenth century, the philosophes were, in Condillac's words, "explaining facts by facts,"[61] they were walking a trail that Newton had blazed. Their buoyant conviction that they were the party of the future was controlled by their recognition that the risks of their campaign were no less immense than its dimensions. The shape of that future seemed uncertain and heavily clouded to the most self-assured among them.

Freud was a latter-day philosophe on this issue as on so many others. To his mind, psychoanalysis was still a young science, requiring much further research; it had barely scratched the surface of mental structures and mental functioning. He liked to say that it had dealt man's narcissism the most consequential

60. Turgot to Buffon, October 1748. Anne-Robert-Jacques Turgot, baron d'Aulne, *Oeuvres de Turgot et documents le concernant,* ed. G. Schelle, 5 vols. (1913–23), I, 111.
61. Condillac, *Traité des systèmes, Oeuvres,* I, 141.

of insults. First Copernicus had attacked that narcissism by demoting man's abode, the earth, from the center of the universe; then Darwin had reduced proud man to the status of an animal. Now, Freud had demonstrated that reason is not master in its own house.[62] He could not exempt psychoanalysis from his sober appraisal of reason's place in man's mental economy. There were some discoveries of which he felt sure: the shibboleths (as he provocatively called them) of psychoanalysis— the underlying orderliness of the mind, the dynamic unconscious, the work of repression, the Oedipus complex, the sexual etiology of the neuroses. Acceptance or rejection of these theories defined to Freud's satisfaction just who could, and who could not, be properly called a psychoanalyst. But across the years, over and over, he worked to get more, and asked his co-workers to supply more, clinical information on paranoia, on female sexuality, and on the other great puzzles of mind. He was persuaded that science in general is a modern venture and had so far solved few of the central riddles of nature.[63] No doubt, psychoanalysis was of necessity in the same leaky boat. Since reason is anything but omnipotent, it followed that its victory, though one might hope for it, must be very far off. It was a flickering lantern in the darkness of the general superstition, prejudice, and ignorance. "Our god logos," Freud

62. See "Eine Schwierigkeit der Psychoanalyse" (1917), *GW* XII, 3–12 / "A Difficulty in the Path of Psycho-Analysis," *SE* XVII, 135–44. Is it a coincidence, or had Freud read Du Bois-Reymond's paper on "Darwin and Kopernicus" (1883), in which he calls Darwin "the Copernicus of the organic world"? Du Bois-Reymond, *Reden*, II, 244.

63. See for one instance, *Zukunft einer Illusion*, *GW* XIV, 379 / *Future of an Illusion*, *SE* XXI, 55.

wrote, "is perhaps not very almighty, can fulfill only a small part of what his predecessors have promised."[64]

In a late letter to Stefan Zweig, Freud returned to that vast uncharted continent awaiting the venturesome psychoanalyst: "Doubt, indeed," he observed, "is inseparable from research, and surely we have not got hold of more than a little fragment of the truth."[65] But all these sincere declarations of modesty were not invitations to gloom or to passivity. Freud thought them to be, rather, invitations to effectiveness. The psychoanalyst's god logos is not omnipotent, but he is infinitely superior to all other deities. When it came to reason (if I may once again borrow a metaphor from theology), Freud the specialist in unreason was a monotheist. All other self-styled divinities promised what they could never possibly deliver; they were impostors. Logos, the divinity of psychoanalysis, promised far less and delivered far more.

This tough-minded devotion to science in contrast to all the other presumptuous guides to knowledge informs the concluding sentences of Freud's *Future of an Illusion*: "No, our science is no illusion. But an illusion it would be to believe that we could get anywhere else what it cannot give us."[66] We may read all of Freud's writings on religion as a commentary on these famous lines. Nothing can be more pointed than their placement and their economy. The scientific world view, he

64. Ibid., 378 / 54.
65. Freud to Stefan Zweig, October 17, 1937. By permission of Sigmund Freud Copyrights, Wivenhoe.
66. *Zukunft einer Illusion, GW* XIV, 380 / *Future of an Illusion, SE* XXI, 56.

notes, apart from its emphasis on the real world, has essentially negative traits. But negative as they are, they give it a decisive advantage over all its rivals: "To content oneself with the truth, to reject illusions."[67] Here, once again, Freud insists on the irreparable split between science and religion: religious doctrines "are not precipitates of experience or end results of thought; they are illusions, fulfillments of the oldest, strongest, most urgent wishes of mankind; the secret of their strength is the strength of these wishes."[68] Religion, in short, is the mother, the champion, and the beneficiary of illusions. To reject their spurious benefits is therefore to reject religion itself. Freud saw no other choice, no possibility of compromise.

Nor had his ancestors, the philosophes. It is true that the Deists postulated a divinity who had set the world in motion and endowed it with a catalogue of physical and moral laws to be discovered and obeyed. But even the Deists thought a workable accommodation with theology an absurdity, and the skeptics and atheists among the philosophes were, if anything, even more reluctant to negotiate. Leibniz might publish a "Dissertation on the Conformity of Faith with Reason," but for the philosophes, such conformity was a fantasy, a pious wish parading as a serious argument. Not even their much-admired John Locke, in search of a truce between the Christian religion and rational philosophy, could escape the philosophes' censure.

67. "Über eine Weltanschauung," *Neue Folge der Vorlesungen, GW* XV, 197 / "Question of a Weltanschauung," *New Introductory Lectures, SE* XXII, 182.

68. *Zukunft einer Illusion, GW* XIV, 352 / *Future of an Illusion, SE* XXI, 30.

After reading Locke's *The Reasonableness of Christianity,* Voltaire jotted into his notebook in his quaint English: "Mr. Lock's reasonableness of Christian relligion is really a new relligion."[69] When the abbé de La Bletterie, a pious French biographer of the emperor Julian the Apostate, called for a "philosophical theologian," Gibbon derisively called such a being a "strange centaur."[70]

Freud had no use for such centaurs. What he wanted to do, and thought psychoanalysis supremely equipped to do, was to expose them as mythical beings so that the work of science might proceed unimpeded. It was as a science that psychoanalysis was "untendentious, except for this: to research and to help."[71] No theology, and virtually no philosophy, could make that claim. In 1928, Freud told Pfister that he took the "abrupt breaking off, not of analytic but of scientific thinking, when it comes to God and Christ, as one of the logically untenable inconsistencies of life, comprehensible only on psychological grounds."[72] He was resigned to such inconsistencies but thought them fatal to the scientific enterprise. Freud, no doubt, was one of those who, in William James's words, "never are, and possibly never under any circumstances could be, converted. Religious ideas cannot become the centre of their spiritual energy." Freud belonged to that crowd of unbelievers

69. *Voltaire's Notebooks,* ed. Theodore Besterman, 2 vols. continuously paginated (1952), 45.

70. Quoted in Shelby T. McCloy, *Gibbon's Hostility to Christianity* (1933), 37.

71. Freud to Ferenczi, April 20, 1919. Freud-Ferenczi Correspondence, Freud Collection, LC.

72. Freud to Pfister, November 25, 1928. *Freud-Pfister,* 135.

with, again in James's words, a certain "inaptitude for religious faith . . . deficient in that category of sensibility."[73]

But what James saw as a grievous flaw, Freud cherished as a valued asset. James had felt sorry for atheists; Freud turned the pity the other way: investigators of religious phenomena who half join the enemy, who become involved in what they should study only from a distance, are afflicted with unconquerable needs.[74] The gratifications such researchers crave in the company of ordinary mortals are gratifications that it was not Freud's desire, or in his gift, to impart. He bowed to the reproaches of his fellowmen, he wrote somberly in *Civilization and Its Discontents,* "that I do not know how to bring them any consolation, for that at bottom they all demand, the wildest revolutionaries no less passionately than the most devout believers."[75] For his own part, science was enough. Writing from ill-provisioned, miserable postwar Vienna in May 1919, he told Ernest Jones, "We are living through a bad time, but science is a mighty power to stiffen one's neck."[76]

73. James, *The Varieties of Religious Experience: A Study in Human Nature* (1902), 204–05.

74. In the psychoanalytic setting, Freud would call such an impermissible engagement countertransference, the analyst's unconscious emotional involvement with his analysand that is likely to ruin the analysis.

75. *Das Unbehagen in der Kultur* (1930), *GW* XIV, 506 / *Civilization and Its Discontents, SE* XXI, 145.

76. Freud to Jones, May 28, 1919, in English. Freud Collection, D2, LC.

✻ TWO

In Search of Common Ground:

"A Better Christian Never Was"

Quite predictably, men of God, whether working pastors or cloistered theologians, took Freud's heresies as so many assaults. And, refusing to turn the other cheek, they struck back. Many of them pointedly ignored Freud altogether, but others took pleasure in identifying him as a symptom. They condemned his views on religion as the characteristic by-product of modern relativism; they thought it impudent for a Jew to venture "a judgment on the Christian faith."[1] In 1928, one anonymous writer, evidently much troubled by what he deplored as the collapse of all moral values in his time, classed Freud's atheism with what he called, a little picturesquely, contemporary "pan-swinism."[2] Delivering the Gifford Lectures in 1939, the year of Freud's death, Reinhold Niebuhr wrote off psychoanalysis as part of the "romantic-materialist revolt" mired in the "cul-de-sac of pessimism."[3] It was open season

1. "Relativism": Emil Pfennigsdorf, *Praktische Theologie*, 2 vols. (1929–30), II, 597; "judgment on Christian faith": Emil Abderhalden, "Sigmund Freuds Einstellung zur Religion," *Ethik*, V (1928–29), 93.

2. Anon., "Psychoanalyse und Religion," *Süddeutsche Monatshefte*, XXV (1928), in A. J. Storfer, "Einige Stimmen zu Sigm. Freuds 'Zukunft einer Illusion,'" *Imago*, XIV (1928), 379.

3. Niebuhr, *The Nature and Destiny of Man: A Christian Interpretation*, 2 vols. (1941, 1943), I, 36, 55.

on Freud, which he had done much to generate and to keep alive.

Rabbis, too, joined the chorus of denunciation. In January 1928, two months after *The Future of an Illusion* was published, the American Reform rabbi Nathan Krass chose to patronize Freud. "In this country," he told his congregation at Temple Emanu-El on New York's Fifth Avenue, "we have grown accustomed to listening to men and women talk on all topics because they have done something notable in one field." There was Edison, who "knows about electricity" and thus finds an audience for his "opinions of theology." Or someone who has made "a name for himself in aviation"—Charles Lindbergh had flown the Atlantic just eight months before—"is asked to make speeches on everything under the sun." Krass's point needed little commentary: "All admire Freud, the psychoanalyst, but that is no reason why we should respect his theology."[4] In his influential *Judaism as a Civilization,* Mordecai Kaplan was even more combative: Freud's "science of religion," he wrote, is "a snare and a delusion." It "presumes to explain away the reality of God" but only manages to confound certain religious dogmas with religion itself in order to discredit it altogether. "That a man of Freud's intellectual caliber should be guilty of confusing 'religion' with a particular type of 'religious doctrines,' is, indeed, a case for psychoanalysis."[5] The preponderant view

4. Krass, January 22, 1928. "Psychoanalyzing the Psychoanalyst," *The New York Times,* January 23, 1928. Quoted in Ronald Clark, *Freud: The Man and the Cause* (1980), 469–70.

5. Mordecai M. Kaplan, *Judaism as a Civilization: Toward a Reconstruction of American-Jewish Life* (1934; ed. 1967), 308–09.

among these students of divinity, Jews and Christians alike, was that Freud's analysis of religion was uninformed, arbitrary, immoral, perhaps neurotic, and yet seductive.

Freud had certainly been provocative enough. But even before the First World War, not long after he had published his first paper on religion, a handful of theologians attempted to repair the rent Freud had made between science and faith. Freud in some measure cooperated with these peacemakers; he gave them a small opening by granting divines a capacity for practicing psychotherapy. He had published his "Obsessive Acts and Religious Practices," in which he saw more than a coincidental resemblance between the rituals of neurotics and those of believers, in 1907. Two years later he told pastor Pfister, at the beginning of their friendship, "You know, our eroticism includes what you call 'love' in your pastoral care—*Seelsorge.*" He added for good measure: "In itself psychoanalysis is neither religious nor the opposite, but an impartial instrument which the minister may employ as much as the layman," provided only that "the liberation of sufferers" is the aim. He professed astonishment that this conciliatory thought should never have occurred to him before. "But that probably happened because to me, the wicked heretic, this whole conceptual sphere is so alien."[6] He was having it both ways: he remained the wicked heretic but was, at the same time, generously proffering the insights of psychoanalysis to men of God. It was an amiable but strictly limited gesture: he found it plausible for a believer to apply psychoanalytic theories and methods to sufferers in his charge—as long as the believer was someone like Pfister.

6. Freud to Pfister, February 9, 1909. *Freud-Pfister,* 12–13 (16–17).

Pfister's encounter with psychoanalysis was the event of his life: Freud gave him the means of resolving a tormenting perplexity—how to help his emotionally disturbed parishioners. Willi Hoffer, an Austrian analyst who knew him well, remembered Pfister as "tall, broad-shouldered," with a "manly mustache" and with "kind and searching eyes."[7] His energies were prodigious, his urge to heal no less so. Born in a suburb of Zurich in 1873, seventeen years Freud's junior, he had experienced his early pastoral work as frustrating and depressing. His father had been a liberal pastor who, anguished by helplessly watching the mortal illness of a young parishioner, had studied medicine so as to function as "physician to the body and the soul at the same time." But he died young, and Oskar Pfister determined to emulate his father's example. He went in quest of an effective "psychology of religion," to discover a cure of souls that none of his reading, none of his colleagues, seemed able to supply. The study of philosophy and of textbooks in psychology brought him no profit; and in 1903, he castigated, in print, "Theology's Sins of Omission Against Modern Psychology."[8] Two years later, he railed indignantly against the impotence of theology and psychology confronted with human suffering.[9] His program, as he put it later, was in place. Early in 1908, he rejected a chair in systematic and practical theology

7. Hoffer, obituary for Pfister, *Int. Jl. of Psycho-Anal.*, XXXIX (1958), 616.

8. See his autobiographical essay in Erich Hahn, ed., *Die Pädagogik der Gegenwart in Selbstdarstellungen,* vol. II (1927), 161–207, esp. 162–67.

9. Pfister's article, "Das Elend unserer wissenschaftlichen Glaubenslehre," appeared in the *Schweizerische theologische Zeitschrift,* XXI (1905), fascicle 4.

to concentrate instead on his mission. A few weeks later, he happened upon Freud's writings, and they struck him with the force of revelation: "I felt," he recalled, "as if old premonitions had become reality." He could not decide whether it was the theoretical or the practical perspective of Freud's work that most attracted him, but he reveled in its realism and its depth: "Here was no interminable speculation about the metaphysics of the soul, no experimenting with minute trifles while the great problems of life remained untouched, no being satisfied with the mere precipitates" of mental life and experience. With Freud, "the highest functions of life stepped before the soul-microscope and gave evidence about their origins and their connections, about the laws of their development, their deeper meaning in the totality of psychic events."[10] Psychoanalysis provided Pfister with the royal road to realizing his vocation. He became the "analyst-pastor-*Analysenpfarrer*" and Freud's friend.[11]

Students of Freud, the godless Jew, must find his untroubled association with Pfister highly instructive. Of all Freud's friendships, some tempestuous and some tranquil, it was distinctly the least expectable and among the most peaceful. In 1909, just as Jung had done three years earlier, Pfister made the opening move by sending Freud an offprint; just as he had with Jung, Freud responded promptly and cordially. He was,

10. Pfister, *Pädagogik der Gegenwart*, 168–70.
11. Hoffer, obituary of Pfister, *Int. Jl. of Psycho-Anal.*, XXXIX (1958), 616.

with both, intent on fostering ties that promised rewards beyond congenial companionship. Jung had given Pfister his first
instruction in psychoanalysis and, as an early member of the
Zurich Freud Society, Pfister was Jung's ally in promoting the
Cause in face of skepticism and derision. Freud did not fail to
inform Pfister that he had "often" heard about him from "our
common friend" Jung, and took pains to convey his "satisfaction" at seeing a pastor dealing analytically with valuable
youthful patients.[12] Late in April 1909, some three months
after he had launched their correspondence, Pfister visited the
Freuds at Berggasse 19. He was an instant success with the
whole family. Many years later, Anna Freud recalled with obvious pleasure the Swiss visitor, visibly a pastor in his sober
appearance and behavior. "In the Freud household, averse to
all religious life," he seemed at first "like an apparition from
an alien world." Evidently, Pfister offered a refreshing change
from the intense, assiduous disciples who usually appeared at
Freud's table, talking analytic shop with their host and neglecting the others. He was humane, cordial, delightful with
the children, "always a welcome guest, in his way a uniquely
human figure."[13] After Pfister and Freud had been friends for
fifteen years, Pfister celebrated their association in the same
warm tones: he had immediately fallen in love, he told Freud,
with the "happy-free spirit" of the whole Freud household.[14]

Freud always retained a last ounce of skeptical distance from
Pfister. For one thing, the pastor's piety, however unconven-

12. Freud to Pfister, January 18, 1909. *Freud-Pfister,* 11 (15).
13. Anna Freud, prefatory remarks to *Freud-Pfister,* 10 (11). Dated 1962.
14. Pfister to Freud, December 30, 1923. Ibid., 94–95 (90–91).

tional and psychoanalytic, kept Freud from investing as much emotion in Pfister as he did, for example, in Ferenczi. In any event, after the emotional bloodletting in which his long, passionate friendship with Fliess had ended, Freud was not disposed to let many other men get close to him. But Pfister confided his most private affairs to Freud: the miseries of his marriage, the obstacles in the way of divorce, the psychological problems of his son. That is the way the friendship matured. But at the outset, Freud was not wholly disinterested; there is something a little manipulative, somewhat suspect, about his quick professions of high regard. For Freud, Pfister was a key that would unlock doors to the outside world, almost as much as Jung. It is not that Freud did not feel at home with Jews— down to the early years of psychoanalysis all his best friends were Jews. But he smarted under the claustrophobic atmosphere of his Viennese psychoanalytic circle. For some years, the small group that had been meeting faithfully at Freud's apartment on Wednesday nights since 1902 was the most parochial of clubs: each of Freud's first followers was a Jew. But none of them impressed him as a plausible successor. Hence Freud greeted his surprising Zurich catches as ambassadors to the world, as recruits who would infuse the Cause with fresh life from outside.

To make psychoanalysis a cosmopolitan affair was high on Freud's agenda. In 1913, embroiled in his crisis with Jung, he told his faithful Berlin adherent Max Eitingon that he could see some advantage in having psychoanalysis confined to "our people." It might provide the kind of strength one gains as one returns to one's "indestructible national feeling." But such reassuring "racial" exclusiveness clashed with Freud's "ideal desires—*Idealwünschen*,"[15] desires for general relevance and general acceptance. And he urgently wanted to see these desires translated into reality. Since his mid-forties, he had fancied himself as failing in health, as a premature geriatric case. As early as 1900, at forty-four, just after he had published his *Interpretation of Dreams*, he called himself, in a letter to Fliess, "an old, somewhat shabby Israelite."[16] He began to look around for someone to preside over his creation. From this rather hypochondriacal vantage point, Freud saw the Swiss who so admired his work as endowed with three negative virtues: they were not old, they were not Viennese, they were not Jewish.

By no means all of Freud's warmth for Jung and Pfister was cool policy: Freud was genuinely fond of Jung for some years and grew ever fonder of Pfister. During the years that Freud's Zurich adherents were sorting themselves out, some to desert him forever, Karl Abraham, his anxious watchdog in Berlin, warned that Pfister was displaying alarming leanings toward Jungian notions.[17] But Freud never wavered in his trust, and though he was susceptible to enthusiasms for newfound friends and often disappointed, this time he was proved right. True, Pfister always retained his intellectual identity: "In music, philosophy, religion," he told Freud, "I walk ways different from yours."[18] But they were ways that Freud could tolerate, even

15. Freud to Eitingon, October 3, 1913. By permission of Sigmund Freud Copyrights, Wivenhoe.

16. Freud to Fliess, May 7, 1900. *Freud-Fliess,* 453 (412).

17. See for instance, Abraham to Freud, July 16, 1914. *Freud-Abraham,* 178 (183).

18. Pfister to Freud, October 21, 1927. *Freud-Pfister,* 117 (110).

in large measure respect. Only in moments of irritation would he admit privately that, "with all his warmth and goodness," Pfister "skirts the ridiculous."[19] But that was in a confidential letter to Max Eitingon.

The friendship between Pfister and Freud survived even *The Future of an Illusion,* which Freud published in 1927, not without some worried glances in the direction of his favorite pastor. Shortly before committing his "brochure" to print, he alerted Pfister that it had "a good deal to do with you. I have been waiting to write it for a long time but pigeonholed it out of consideration for you, until at last the urge became too strong." Asserting once again his "absolutely negative attitude toward religion, in every form and dilution," he feared that the essay "will be painful to you."[20]

Pfister cordially acknowledged Freud's warning and sent a reassuring reply: "An intellectually powerful adversary of religion is surely more useful to it than a thousand useless adherents." He added gracefully, on a personal note, "You were always tolerant toward me, should I not be so toward your atheism?"[21] After reading the little book with care, Pfister tried to define his differences with Freud in the gentlest possible manner: "You know that neither my attitude toward you, nor my pleasure in psychoanalysis, is diminished in the least by

19. Freud to Eitingon, April 3, 1928. By permission of Sigmund Freud Copyrights, Wivenhoe.

20. Freud to Pfister, October 16, 1927. *Freud-Pfister,* 116 (109–10).

21. Pfister to Freud, October 21, 1927. Ibid., 117 (110).

my reservations concerning your rejection of religion. I have always emphasized that psychoanalysis indeed constitutes the most fruitful part of psychology, but never the whole science of the mental, and still less a view of life and the world. Surely you are of the same opinion."[22] Freud was, but drew directly opposed conclusions from it. "I rejoice in all your success," he told Pfister in 1934. "That you are such a convinced analyst and still, at the same time, a clerical gentleman, ranks among the contradictions that make life so interesting."[23] The ability of the educated to combine faith in God with trust in science always astonished Freud a little, and amused him more. In May 1939, a few months before his death, he wrote to a correspondent in Palestine, "The way you are able to reconcile esteem for scientific research with belief in the reliability of the biblical report calls forth my fullest admiration; I could not manage the feat." He wondered a little testily: "But whence do you take the right to monopolize the truth for the Bible? I suppose it simply means: I believe because I believe."[24]

This states the issue with Freud's usual economy; Freud saw Pfister's life's work as a grand, in its way admirable, contradiction in terms. In 1937, in his last extant letter to Pfister, Freud informed him that in a work on Moses and monotheism, as yet unpublished, he would be dealing "once again with religion, for you, too, not agreeable."[25] It could not be wholly

22. Pfister to Freud, November 24, 1927. Ibid., 121–22 (114).
23. Freud to Pfister, November 25, 1934. Ibid., 155 (142).
24. Freud to Rafael da Costa, May 2, 1939. Freud Museum, London.
25. Freud to Pfister, March 27, 1937. *Freud-Pfister,* 157 (144). In a brief correspondence with the Portuguese Baptist Abel de Castro, a teacher and journalist who tried in his ambitious publications to find ways of reconciling

agreeable to Pfister, no matter how tolerant he might show himself with his atheist friend, no matter how grateful he was to Freud for having pointed the way to healing his parishioners. After all, several years before he published his uncompromising paper on the Weltanschauung of psychoanalysis, Freud had already rehearsed one of his favorite ideas in private to Pfister: "Analysis produces no new world view. But it does not need one, for it rests on the general scientific world view with which the religious one remains incompatible."[26]

P fister made his most strenuous effort at reconciling these world views—at least his own and Freud's—when he tried to coopt Freud to the select elite of good Christians. When Freud asked him in that famous letter why the world had had to wait for a godless Jew to create psychoanalysis, Pfister found an astonishing reply. First of all, he informed Freud, "You are no Jew," something that, in view of his unbounded admiration for Jews like Amos, Isaiah, and Jeremiah, Pfister professed to regret. Second, "You are not godless, for whoever lives in God, and whoever battles for the liberation of love remains, according

religion and science, Freud sounded this note again: "I gather you think strictly religious," Freud wrote, in English, "and I am afraid if my relation to religion were known to you your personal attitude towards me would be less friendly." By permission of Sigmund Freud Copyrights, Wivenhoe (this correspondence has been published by Maria Alice Mava do Valle, Orlando Silva Santos, Francisco Alvim, Pedro Luzes, "Four Recently Discovered Letters by Freud to a Portuguese Correspondent. A Contribution to the Pre-History of Psycho-Analysis in Portugal," *Int. Rev. of Psycho-Anal.*, VI [1979], 437–40).

26. Freud to Pfister, February 16, 1929. *Freud-Pfister,* 139 (129).

to John 4.16, in God." This was not precisely the kind of characterization for which Freud was prepared, but Pfister had a final surprise in store: thinking of Freud, he was moved to say, "A better Christian never was."[27] Freud, who could be tactful, passed over this heartfelt compliment in silence.[28]

Pfister's construction of a Christian Freud, though, was no mere empty verbiage or affectionate effusion. It was Pfister's way of saying that he had discovered some substantial affinities between his version of Protestantism and Freud's thought. He interpreted his own religious thought as a positive, practical, psychologically sophisticated faith purged of all superstition and all remnants of primitive ritual. Pfister regretted, he told Freud bluntly, to see Freud reject philosophy and theology with such vehemence. At their best, he believed, both cannot be dismissed as sheer projection.[29] Indeed, his negative, somewhat doctrinaire skepticism, Pfister thought, blinded Freud to the obvious parallels between psychoanalysis and Pfister's Protestantism. Both work to reduce guilt, which they recognize as a kind of punishment for defying authority; both aim to replace

27. Pfister to Freud, October 29, 1918. Ibid., 64 (63). Coming upon this letter years later, Anna Freud quite sensibly found it incomprehensible: "What in the world does Pfister mean here," she wrote to Ernest Jones, "and why does he want to dispute the fact that my father is a Jew, instead of accepting it?" Anna Freud to Ernest Jones, July 12, 1954. Jones Papers, Archives of the British Psycho-Analytical Society, London.

28. Years later Freud commented obliquely on this passage, observing to Pfister that he rather reminded him of the monk who insists on seeing Nathan the Wise, the idealized Jewish sage who is the hero of Lessing's famous dramatized sermon on toleration, as a Christian: "I am far from being Nathan." Freud to Pfister, February 16, 1929. *Freud-Pfister,* 140 (129).

29. See Pfister to Freud, November 24, 1927. Ibid., 121–25 (113–17).

a stern with a kindly father. What is more, both utilize regression as a method of healing: it is no accident that in pastoral care, as in psychoanalysis, the patient becomes as a little child.[30] Most important of all, both Freud's psychoanalysis and Pfister's theology place love at the core of life.

This last argument did not seem farfetched. Like Pfister, Freud had explicitly likened the eroticism of psychoanalysis to the love at the heart of pastoral care.[31] He said much the same thing to Jung, calling psychoanalysis "essentially a cure through love."[32] And he gladly let himself be persuaded that the libido of psychoanalysis closely coincides with the Eros of Plato.[33] Pfister now added Jesus to the short list of Freud's distinguished precursors. Jesus, he wrote, "introduced love into the center of life, into the heart of religion and morality, and with that overcame anxiety and ceremonialism." This argument was a great favorite with Pfister: love is all. Thus he energetically concludes his study of love in children and its

30. See Pfister, "Neutestamentliche Seelsorge und psychoanalytische Therapie," *Imago*, XX (1934), 425–43.

31. But from the beginning, Freud insisted on radically distinguishing his ideas from Pfister's: "I have, as you admit," he told Pfister in 1910, "done a great deal for love, but that it rests on the ground of all things I cannot confirm from my experience, except if one (which is psychologically correct) adds in hatred." Freud to Pfister, March 17, 1910. *Freud-Pfister,* 33–34 (36).

32. Freud to Jung, December 6, 1906. *Freud-Jung,* 13 (12–13).

33. See "Vorwort" to the fourth edition of *Drei Abhandlungen zur Sexualtheorie* (1920), *GW* V, 32 / "Preface," *Three Essays on the Theory of Sexuality, SE* VII, 134, citing an article by Max Nachmansohn, "Freuds Libidotheorie verglichen mit der Eroslehre Platos," *Int. Z. für Psychoanal.,* III (1915), 65–83.

aberrations with the glowing affirmation, in capitals, "ONLY LOVE CAN LEAD TO LOVE."[34] He was bound to acknowledge that Platonic, Freudian, and Christian love substantially diverge, but took comfort from what they have in common.[35] Certainly he did not delude himself that Freud was on the verge of accepting baptism. But in celebrating true love as desire purged through sublimation, he welcomed Freud to Jesus's camp: a better Christian never was.

This radical, rather simplistic reading of Jesus added force to Pfister's critique of Roman Catholicism. "With its dualist morality," he wrote in 1910, "Catholicism is a religion of the maximal repression of natural instinctual life." After all, "its ideal is the monk, who renounces woman, personal independence, and 'the world.'" Many saints had been admirably moral and devout, but at best they had sublimated their drives incompletely. "It is not only that they suffer almost without exception from patent neuroses, visions, anesthesias, anxiety states, obsessions, hysterical pains, disturbances of consciousness, pathological narrowing of the mental range of vision;" but "*very often cruelly mistreated sexuality*" also lamentably disfigures their lives. In salutary contrast, "Protestantism has accomplished, starting from its religious-ethical feeling, what the psychoanalyst strives for on the basis of scientific insight. It reverses the phenomenon of repression formed in celibacy,

34. Pfister, *Die Frömmigkeit des Grafen Ludwig von Zinzendorf* (1910; 2d ed., 1925), 114; *Love in Children and Its Aberrations: A Book for Parents and Teachers* (1922; tr. Eden and Cedar Paul, 1924), 555.

35. For one such admission, see *Christianity and Fear: A Study in the History and in the Psychology and Hygiene of Religion* (1944; tr. W. H. Johnston, 1948), 184.

hierarchy, and monastic life." In Pfister's enthusiastic and partisan analysis, the Protestant ideals of Christian marriage and the priesthood of all believers counteract the ravages of the "father complex." This is the message of Jesus to the world; he had brought forth "the sunrise of a new life in joy, freedom, health."[36]

It is an intriguing and startling picture: Jesus, not Freud, the first psychoanalyst. It is, too, a highly original way for a Protestant to say harsh things about Roman Catholics. But Pfister was no less severe with Protestant sects like the Pietists, whose sentimental religiosity of the heart deeply offended him. Analyzing the piety of Count Zinzendorf, the most prominent of eighteenth-century Pietist activists in the German states and the American colonies, he objected to his sadistic, homoerotic disparagement of worldly conjugal love. Zinzendorf had preached an intense devotion to the blood and the wounds of Christ. This led, Pfister noted severely, to "the ugliest sexualization of religion" and to "religious orgies."[37] That was the kind of psychoanalytic dissection that Freud could applaud— the anticlericalism of the clerical. After reading Pfister's manuscript on Count Zinzendorf with unfeigned approval, he praised it as "excellently limpid to the last, impressive, persuasive to everyone who does not want to keep from being persuaded at all costs."[38] About Pfister's campaign to conquer him for Christianity Freud was rather less enthusiastic.

36. Pfister, "Die Psychoanalyse als wissenschaftliches Prinzip und als seelsorgerische Methode," *Evangelische Freiheit*, X (1910), 196–97.
37. See Pfister, *Die Frömmigkeit des Grafen Zinzendorf,* 116, 107.
38. Freud to Pfister, June 17, 1910. *Freud-Pfister,* 39 (41).

In his search for a common ground between liberal theology and psychoanalysis, Pfister could never take the majority of divines with him. He was treading a largely unmarked path and, as the censoriousness of his Swiss colleagues to his departures from orthodoxy amply demonstrates, a hazardous one. "The theologians," he recalled some years later, "could not approve of my daring to investigate the life of faith in its immediate reality, instead of merely grubbing around in books." It did not surprise him "that my scientific reputation, hitherto spotless, collapsed as soon as I advocated psychoanalytic research. The well-meaning, feeling sorry for me, worried and gently reproachful, asked me why I should have acted so irresponsibly." After the Breslau Congress of Psychologists in 1913 had warned against "the excesses of 'youth-psychoanalysis,'" Pfister was subjected to what he called "a smear campaign probably unprecedented in the history of pedagogy."[39]

But he was not alone or desperately eccentric. "Theological Freud-*Schwärmerei*" had to wait until after Freud's death. Then a few clerics came to describe him as a great scientist whom the theologian is bound to respect, or, even more extravagantly, as a "gift of God to man."[40] Even in his lifetime, the tribe of Freud's sympathizers among theologians had been growing. To judge from some of Pfister's unpublished letters to Freud, from

39. Pfister, *Pädagogik der Gegenwart*, 171–72. In fairness he adds that his "most vehement adversaries, not to say: enemies," were not the theologians but the experimental psychologists.

40. See Joachim Scharfenberg, *Sigmund Freud und seine Religionskritik als Herausforderung für den christlichen Glauben* (1968; 3d ed., 1971), 29.

the early 1920s on, schools of divinity were eager to have Pfister lecture on the religious implications of psychoanalysis, or at least on the clinical uses of psychoanalysis for the cure of souls. "Today," he informed Freud in 1921, "I participated in a meeting in which two professors of theology warmly championed the indispensability of psa. for historical-critical theology."[41] Again, that same year, "A few days ago I returned from a trip to Germany. In Koblenz and Nürnberg I gave lectures to pastors about psa. and encountered as much interest as ignorance."[42] A few years later, in 1927, he was asked to lecture to the theological faculty at Birmingham.[43] The cause of Freud was visibly gaining converts among men of God.

This was the atmosphere in which Cyril Forster Garbett, bishop of Southwark, could argue that "there is no necessary conflict between religion and psychology. Christianity is not opposed either to psychology or to the New Psychology." This did not, of course, mean that the bishop embraced psychoanalysis. He admitted that it espoused some ideas clearly unacceptable to a believer. Certainly "the conflict" between Christian faith and materialistic psychology "is with some psychological theories which are connected with the New Psychology." But there was hope for that psychology, nevertheless, for these theories "certainly are not essential to it."[44] And other

41. Pfister to Freud, March 14, 1921. By permission of Sigmund Freud Copyrights, Wivenhoe.

42. Pfister to Freud, October 24, 1921. By permission of Sigmund Freud Copyrights, Wivenhoe.

43. Pfister to Freud, May 6, 1927. By permission of Sigmund Freud Copyrights, Wivenhoe.

44. Cyril Forster Garbett, "Introduction" to O. Hardman, ed., *Psychology and the Church* (1925), xi.

pious writers were still more forthcoming: in 1936, G. Simpson Marr, a specialist in the medical implications of Christianity, declared in a historical survey of sex in religion that "the genius of Freud will abide permanently in his influence on mankind," even if it should turn out that he had added "no single permanent truth" to "the world of knowledge." For, "right or wrong," Freud "has forced us all to dig more critically, explore more candidly into human morals and human conduct; he has helped to break down shams by tearing away its cloak of shame," especially in regard to "infantile sexuality and the ravages of repression."[45]

Paul Tillich, a far more considerable theologian and publicist, in his late years downright fashionable, made much of this argument. In 1929 he observed that, following the lead of Nietzsche and the great late-nineteenth-century novelists, psychoanalysis had "brought to light the mechanisms of repression in the bourgeois Protestant personality and the explosive re-emergence of the vital (unconscious) forces."[46] Tillich saw Freud and his companions as unmaskers, bound to arouse resistance. In their work they had helped to rescue theology from becoming a marginal discipline.[47] If modern theology had turned out to be anything more than a footnote to culture, Tillich thought that Freud was largely responsible.

45. Marr, *Sex in Religion: An Historical Survey* (1936), 194–96.
46. Tillich, "The Idea and the Ideal of Personality" (1929), in Tillich, *The Protestant Era* (tr. James Luther Adams, 1951), 148–49. I should perhaps note that in presenting his sweeping, rather undifferentiated history of the modern European mind, Tillich was inclined to define "psychoanalysis" rather broadly.
47. Storfer, "Einige Stimmen zu Freuds 'Zukunft einer Illusion,'" 378.

This was weighty praise, but he had more to say. Temperamentally disposed to discover large, systematic connections among phenomena, Tillich was not content with merely recognizing the utility of psychoanalysis in cultural criticism or pastoral practice. He preferred to enlist it in the great tradition of struggle against rationalism, which reached back to Duns Scotus, Paracelsus, and Luther. Modern history, to Tillich's mind, had witnessed "the victory of the philosophy of consciousness over the philosophy of the unconscious, irrational will," an unfortunate evolution epitomized by Calvinism, Descartes, and oppressive American religiosity. "But in spite of this victory, the protest was not silenced." The impressive cavalcade of objectors including Pascal, Kierkegaard, Marx, Dostoevsky, Rimbaud, Baudelaire, to say nothing of Kafka or of Bergson, with his *élan vital,* had prepared "the ground for what was to follow in the twentieth century," with Freud in the vanguard—a stunning and incongruous intellectual pedigree that leaves the historian gasping for breath. Freud's discoveries about the unconscious had been known "for many decades and even centuries" and had been used "to fight the victorious philosophy of consciousness. What Freud did was to give this protest a scientific methodological foundation."[48] Psychoanalysis and some types of philosophy, then, are inseparable: they are doing the same cultural work. Thus Tillich joined what Freud had spent his life trying to keep asunder.

The alliance between psychoanalysis and philosophy seemed

48. See "The Theological Significance of Existentialism and Psychoanalysis" (1955), in Tillich, *Theology of Culture,* ed. Robert C. Kimball, 112–25.

to Tillich most visible in the existentialist movement of his time: "Psychoanalysis and existentialism have been connected with each other from the very beginning; they have mutually influenced each other in the most radical and profound way." Both seek to describe "man's existential predicament," his "estranged existence." For all his heroic, highly imaginative labor at assimilation, Tillich recognized some "basic" differences between psychoanalysis and existentialism. While the latter "speaks of the universal human situation," the former concentrates on those who "try to escape the situation by fleeing into neurosis and falling into psychosis." Worse, many of Freud's followers have abandoned his deepest existential insights, and Freud, too, had failed to secure ultimate clarity about human nature; his "pessimism about the nature of man and his optimism about the possibilities of healing were never reconciled in him or his followers." But setting these reservations aside, Tillich maintained that Freud's ideas have yielded an impressive harvest for theology: Freud remains "the most profound of all the depth psychologists." Psychoanalysis has rediscovered long-neglected deep mental material and sin (not "sins," but "tragic estrangement"), and it has championed "grace" and "forgiveness" against a "pharisaic moralism."[49] In the history of attempts to rescue psychoanalysis for religion, Tillich's speculative ecumenical effort must stand as among the most daring and most acrobatic any theologian has ever undertaken.

49. Ibid., 119–21. Tillich's charge that Freud was a therapeutic optimist would have astonished Freud.

Few other theologians were quite so global or quite so supportive of Freud's thought as Tillich. A more characteristic way of asserting affinities between psychoanalysis and religion was to denigrate Freud as unoriginal. No doubt (so runs the argument) his ideas contain some truth, but they had in fact been discovered earlier and stated better by Christians. Reinhold Niebuhr for one thought that "modern psychoanalysts might learn much about the basic character of anxiety and its relation to human freedom from the greatest of Christian psychologists, Søren Kierkegaard."[50] Some critics employed this tactic in somewhat less condescending tones. "No one today," wrote the devout Swiss physician Paul Tournier, contests the reality "of the mechanisms by which feelings of guilt are aroused, nor the importance of Freud's discovery." But that discovery "only confirms what the Bible had already told us— how much the human being needs to feel loved."[51] Otto A.

50. Niebuhr, *Nature and Destiny of Man*, I, 45n–46n.

51. Tournier, *Guilt and Grace: A Psychological Study* (1958; tr. Arthur W. Heathcote and others, 1962), 63. In another characteristic homiletic text, Tournier takes a rather more severe view, weighing Freud the discoverer in the balance and finding him sadly wanting. He attributes to Freud the attempt (made in company with Rousseau, Nietzsche, and Marx) at freeing humanity from guilt, which is equivalent to freeing it from convictions. *The Whole Person in a Broken World* (1947; tr. John and Helen Doberstein, 1965), 24. Tournier brings himself to admit that "we are grateful to [Freud] for his scientific work," but, he immediately adds, "we must recognize, on the other hand, that there is no necessary connection between his scientific contributions and the philosophical views which he believed he must deduce from it. In his scientific work he was a genius who cast a brilliant light upon the psychological mechanisms that occur in the unconscious, what his disciple Dr. Charles Odier calls 'functions,' as distinguished from 'values.' And yet

Piper, who after a distinguished career in Europe moved to Princeton University as professor of theology, observed that Freud's psychology is "one sided in its belief in the omnipotence of sex, but unsurpassed in its study of the subconscious operation of sexual motives in all spheres of human life." Unsurpassed, but not unanticipated: Freud's analysis "confirms the Christian contention that in a sinful life[,] sex life is full of abysses and incomprehensibilities and constantly beset by dangers to which people succumb unawares." Compared to the depth of Christian perception, Piper thought, psychoanalysis sheds only a faint, largely borrowed light on human nature: St. Paul's understanding of "sexual sins shows the insight of a man nineteen hundred years before the discovery of psychoanalysis, an insight which probed more deeply than the latter into the ramifications and abysses of human nature."[52] This was a safe, comfortable way of domesticating psychoanalysis: to draw its fangs, trumpet its merits, and evade its subversiveness.

Over the past several decades, pious publicists have made these views commonplace. In 1956, an English physician, W. Earl Biddle, summarized them with admirable economy in a little treatise optimistically titled *Integration of Religion and Psychiatry*: "Freud believed that he had disproved the reality of

---

subsequently he maintained that all spiritual values, religion, morality, poetry, are to be reduced to these functions. . . . In this way Freud came to deny all value" (87–88). In this analysis, Tournier forces Freud into some ill-assorted company: "We can regard Communism, Nazism, existentialism, or Freudianism as symptoms of a profound illness of the world, but also as signs of its reaction against this illness" (89–90).

52. Piper, *The Christian Interpretation of Sex* (1942), 213–14, 18.

God, but his appreciation of religious values may be surprising to some who have misunderstood him." Biddle did not hesitate to declare "Freud's materialistic philosophy" to be "untenable" but was glad to acknowledge that "his psychoanalytic discoveries cannot be summarily dismissed as irreligious and pernicious." Indeed, "when the truth in Freud's discoveries is brought to light it will be found that they do not conflict with religious principles. To the contrary, Freud discovered that man is by nature religious and that the concept of the Supreme Being is *experienced* in childhood." In short, "Freud's basic quarrel was not with *religion,* but with religious *dogma.*"[53]

The discovery of common ground between faith and psychoanalysis has been made again and again. Perhaps its most energetic and sophisticated spokesman has been R. S. Lee, an Anglican divine well grounded in psychoanalysis. Lee escapes condescension and apologetics to plead for cooperation between theologians and psychoanalysts on the basis of compatibility rather than some fancied identity. The popular notion of psychoanalysis as handmaiden to religion, able to "cleanse Christianity of non-Christian elements," is still in evidence in his book, but Lee's ambitions are greater than this. Believing in both Christ and Freud, he voices his conviction that they are reconcilable.[54]

To uphold his doctrine of separate, equal, and mutually useful spheres, Lee seeks from the outset to discredit the old

53. Biddle, *Integration of Religion and Psychiatry* (1956), 1–2, ix, 2. This is, of course, what Freud's nephew Harry Freud said when he called his uncle antireligious but by no means an atheist.

54. Lee, *Freud and Christianity* (1948; ed. 1967), 9.

chestnut of an irreparable conflict between religion and science. The Fundamentalists have been consistently wrong on matters of fact: the literal truth of Genesis is certainly indefensible. But such Christian stories as the Creation are parables and myths, valid in their own right. In short, science has its proper domain; it establishes facts, while religion constructs an order of values. It follows that mutual toleration is rational and indispensable. William James, we know, had taken that position around the turn of the century.

Cunningly adapting Freud's account of psychological development to the mission of Christianity, Lee tries to show that the psychoanalytic accounts of mental structure, of the unconscious and the death drive, all point the way to a purified, psychoanalytic Christianity. Christians must develop "a new theology of Heaven, one that will do justice to the life instinct."[55] Analysis can do even more: it can clarify the believer's relations to his church as mother and his God as father and overcome the perils of a guilt-ridden, superego religion. Lee extols Freud as Christianity's great modern teacher. "Two of the chief marks of a Christian are freedom and love. Psychoanalysis shows that they cannot be produced by what I have called Super-ego religion, with its emphasis on sin, guilt, and punishment—its castration complex." Adapting Freud's famous definition of the aims of psychoanalytic therapy—"Where id was, there ego shall be"—Lee concludes: "Freedom does not mean freedom only of the Ego. . . . It means that the Id, Ego and Super-Ego are all able to gain more effective expression

55. Ibid., 98.

because they have found the right relationships with each other through the leadership of the Ego."[56] This is an astonishing reversal: psychoanalysis, the handmaiden of religion, has become its master and standard. Lee borrows the litmus paper separating sound from spurious religion from the godless Jew Freud himself.[57]

The Jewish response to Freud's dissection of religion, like the Christian response, occupied a wide spectrum: silence, rejection, condescension, approval, appropriation. Most rabbis, Jewish theologians, and learned Jewish journals assiduously ignored psychoanalysis and the problems it posed for faith: the way that the *Jewish Quarterly Review,* for one, virtually blocked out Freud exhibits this determined defensiveness. In the mid-1950s, Robert L. Katz, by no means an unsympathetic observer, summed up Freud's contribution to Jewish thought as insignificant: "Freud's own studies of religion," he noted, have had "little creative influence on Judaism, and have, in fact, evoked no little resistance to psychoanalytic speculation in problems of Jewish history and theology."[58] Nor has the situation markedly changed since. Certainly, as far as the two most

56. Ibid., 154, 161.

57. I take this point from Scharfenberg, who has lucidly objected, "With this, [Lee] turns the decisive question of theology, what is to be considered Christian and un-Christian, over to psychopathology. His equation runs: un-Christian = immature-neurotic; Christian = mature-healthy." *Freud und seine Religionskritik,* 32.

58. Katz, reprint of "Aspects of Pastoral Psychology and the Rabbinate," from *Pastoral Psychology,* V (October 1954), 7 unnumbered pages.

seminal Jewish thinkers of our century, Franz Rosenzweig and
Martin Buber, were concerned, Freud might well not have
lived. Rosenzweig, as scattered entries in his journals and comments in his letters attest, was interested in Freud; he had read
Totem and Taboo, was familiar with Freud's dream theory and
the Oedipus complex, but psychoanalysis left no precipitate on
his writings.[59] Buber for his part detested Freud; early and late
in his life, he intended to write a refutation of psychoanalysis.[60]
There has been no Jewish R. S. Lee, let alone a Paul Tillich.

Not unexpectedly, the resistance has at times reached the
extreme of shrill denunciation. Dr. Martin Kushner, writing
from a devout Jewish perspective, denounced Freud in 1967 as
a "fiction writer" responsible for much gibberish. "All this talk
of Freud" about infantile sexuality "is an unintelligible bab-
ble."[61] Again not unexpectedly, Kushner peppered his exercise
in name-calling with the religious metaphors that have proved

59. Thus, see the entry in his *Tagebuch,* under date of April 4, 1922.
Franz Rosenzweig, *Briefe und Tagebücher,* ed. Rachel Rosenzweig and Edith
Rosenzweig-Scheinmann, with collaboration of Bernhard Casper, 2 vols.
(1979), II, 770; and his letter to Ernst Simon, December 18, 1926. Ibid.,
1114.

60. See Grete Schaeder, in Martin Buber, *Briefwechsel aus sieben Jahrzehnten,* ed. Schaeder, 3 vols. (1972–75), I, 37, 94. See also Buber to Martin
Gerson, August 30, 1928, ibid., II, 322, and to Maurice Friedman,
December 12, 1956, ibid., III, 403. Probably the most respectable reader
of Freud I have encountered among the rabbis was the cultivated Conservative
rabbi Milton Steinberg, who liked to quote Ruskin and Pater and T. S. Eliot
in his sermons, and who on occasion alluded appreciatively to "modern
psychology," and even to "the Freudian psychology." See esp. "Inviting the
North Wind" and "If the Dead Come Back: A Post-yizkor Fantasy," in
Bernard Mandelbaum, ed., *From the Sermons of Rabbi Milton Steinberg: High
Holydays and Major Festivals* (1954), 176, 198.

61. Kushner, *Freud—A Man Obsessed* (1967), 17, 47.

such an obstruction to a balanced reading of Freud's work: "The priesthood of Freud's cult, as a vested interest, tries to strengthen and perpetuate itself, not unlike any other vested interest. In this lies the evil influence of Freud on society."[62] What particularly worried Kushner was Freud's corrosive effect on moral standards: "Freud rescues the homosexual, Lesbian, pederast, sadist, and masochist from the public stigma of being called sexual pervert and gives them status as being a 'natural kind.' This whitewashing of sexual perversions is one of the basic concepts of Freud's psychoanalysis."[63]

Freud's presumed indifference, indeed antagonism, to necessary morality has continued to agitate pious Jews in the decades after his death. In 1976, Avrohom Amsel, an orthodox rabbi and social worker, armoring himself with endorsements from eminent Jewish divines in Israel and the United States, pitted the ethical Jewish approach to the study of mind derived from Torah and Talmud against the nonethical psychoanalytic approach. The cause of emotional turmoil, Amsel says flatly, is sin, but Freud and Freudianism absolve the sinner as merely sick. Amsel agreed with Kushner that the consequences for society must be nothing less than calamitous.[64] This charge has proved a fertile field for denunciation. More recently, in 1979, Joel Klein of the Institute of Child Study at Toronto, confronting psychoanalysis with the Torah, denounced the former as a fatal subversion of the latter. Freud's teaching, Klein

62. Ibid., 138.
63. Ibid., 41.
64. Amsel, *Rational Irrational: Man Torah Psychology* (1976); see also his earlier *Judaism and Psychology* (1969).

persuaded himself, essentially amounts to a "whittling away at
the client's conscience."[65] Worse, "Freud introduced the antireligious attitude into psychotherapy with a vehemence. Ar-
bitrarily he attributed many social problems to religious causes
and actively fought against the religious convictions of his
clients. These prejudices he recorded with pride in his journals."[66] It should scarcely be necessary to point out that this
indictment draws on largely fictitious evidence: Freud certainly
did not fight against the religious convictions of his "clients,"
or note them in his journal.

Other Jewish critics of Freud's thought have shown themselves less imaginative and less excited, but they have been no
less appalled at the threat of psychoanalysis to the moral cer-
tainties that hold societies together. In the early 1960s
Stuart E. Rosenberg of Toronto, then rabbi of the largest Jewish
congregation in Canada, genially commended the "Freudian
revolution" for coming "at the right time and for the right
place," and for making "positive," indeed "large and massive,"
contributions "to our understanding of man's mental functioning."[67] At the same time, Rosenberg reproached "orthodox
Freudians" for destroying man's conscience in the bud, and
lectured them on freedom which "does not consist of the absence of rules and the lack of personal discipline." Calmly
disregarding the overpowering evidence in Freud's writings, he
concluded that "it was conscience, of course, which annoyed

65. Klein, *Psychology Encounters Judaism* (1979), 8.
66. Ibid., 9.
67. Rosenberg, *More Loves than One: The Bible Confronts Psychiatry* (1963),
22, 25.

Freud, no end; it came too close to being a spiritual quality."[68]
Reading such material—and there are ample supplies—I am
reminded of a review that Charles Beard wrote many years ago
charging that the book he had just read had been written
without fear and without research.

Confronting this array of angry and anxious Jewish critics
of Freud, more irenic Jewish voices have remained, precisely
like their Christian counterparts, in a minority. But in recent
years this minority has grown increasingly vocal, aided by the
widespread pressure to make the rabbinate into one of the
"helping professions." While "clinical pastoral psychology,"
one well-informed observer noted in the 1950s, "has received
relatively little attention in the rabbinate,"[69] the rabbinate has
not remained wholly immune. The call for at least a modicum
of psychological sophistication has begun to infect the Jewish
clergy, producing sincere efforts to find at least some value in
Freud's writings. Much of this modern pastoral psychology has

68. Ibid., 44, 109. While Rosenberg's tone is, as we have seen, far from
wholly hostile, he gave at least some of his most determined anti-Freudian
readers highly satisfying comfort. Thus the eminent Reform rabbi and Zionist
Abba Hillel Silber praised Rosenberg's book on the jacket as "sound, scholarly, unimpressed by the biologically deterministic philosophies and the
pseudo-scientific psycho-analytical notions of our day." At the same time,
Silber was not wholly certain of his anti-Freudian stance. Thus, in his *Where
Judaism Differed: An Inquiry into the Distinctiveness of Judaism* (1961), he could
write: "The new sciences of psychoanalysis and psychotherapy are based on
the theory that man can be helped to change his life, his attitudes, his
conduct, and hence his destiny, once he is given new insights and a clearer
understanding of himself, his history, and his capacity." These two new
sciences are (or were in 1961) for Silber welcome escape routes from fatalism
(see p. 252). Perhaps Emerson was right: consistency may indeed be the
hobgoblin of little minds.

69. Katz, "Aspects of Pastoral Psychology and the Rabbinate."

remained, quite deliberately, highly eclectic, yoking such in-congruous company as Erich Fromm and Martin Buber with Sigmund Freud.[70] A few Jewish publicists laboring to redefine the respective tasks of psychoanalysis and religion have taken their stand on the familiar, relatively safe ground of separate if congenial spheres. Pfister, who had advertised his liberal psychoanalytic Protestantism as the most suitable theology for the absorption of Freud's ideas, has received in these last years some serious competition from Reform Jews.[71]

It was Rabbi Joshua Loth Liebman who showed in the 1940s, not long after Freud's death, how active and effective this com-petition could become. Liebman was a cultural phenomenon more than a serious thinker. A graduate of Hebrew Union College in Jewish philosophy, he became rabbi of the Reform Temple Israel in Boston, served as university preacher in Ivy League colleges, made himself into a widely heard radio preacher over national networks, and published, in 1946, at

70. For one such instance, see Robert L. Katz, "Becoming a Friend to Myself: With a Little Help from Sigmund Freud, Erich Fromm, and Martin Buber," in Edward A. Goldman, ed., *Jews in a Free Society: Challenges and Opportunities* (1978), 84–102. For Katz's eclecticism at work, see his *Empathy: Its Nature and Uses* (1963).

71. One such instance has been Abraham N. Franzblau, a physician and prominent pastoral psychiatrist. The "areas of mutual potentiality for aiding mankind" in psychiatry and religion, he wrote in 1956, are "destined" to "increase as the practitioners in the two fields come to understand each other better and work more closely together." Indeed, the border between will lengthen, and both "may derive" from this "greater strength and effective-ness." He thought this "truer of Judaism, by and large, than of most other religions, and truest of the liberal wings within Judaism, where the conflicts between psychoanalytic and religious doctrines are less than elsewhere." Franzblau in Simon Noveck, ed., *Judaism and Psychiatry: Two Approaches to the Personal Problems and Needs of Modern Man* (1956), 191–92.

the age of thirty-nine, his astonishing best-seller *Peace of Mind*. The country seemed parched for it: the book garnered respectful endorsements, ecstatic reviews, and vast sales. In 1966, twenty years after its publication, *Peace of Mind* was in its fortieth printing, with more than 900,000 sold and millions of readers uplifted. Liebman died prematurely, of a heart ailment, in 1948, but not before he had witnessed his awesome popularity.

The message Liebman preached to the world was one of relentless hope. His widow reported that he liked to call himself a "provisional optimist."[72] But this is too tentative a self-appraisal. For Liebman, human beings are essentially good, and when they go astray, repressing their feelings and suffering shipwreck in love, they may be healed, healed by Freudian psychology. For Liebman, writing just after the Second World War, Freud "has been the supreme cartographer of consciousness, the first scientist to draw a truly helpful map of the terrain of the psyche."[73] To him Freud was the modern psychologist par excellence: "dynamic psychology" had been "created by Freud," who had proved "the shrewdest analyst of our civilization and its disorders."[74] Freely displaying his respect for the Founder, Liebman sprinkled his pages with technical psychoanalytic terms: repression, narcissism, identification. True, Mrs. Liebman insisted that her late husband had not been

72. Fan Loth Liebman, "Preface" (dated 1965) to Joshua Loth Liebman, *Hope for Man: An Optimistic Philosophy and Guide to Self-Fulfillment* (1966), 8.
73. Joshua Loth Liebman, "A Creative Partnership," in Liebman, ed., *Psychiatry and Religion* (1948), 27.
74. Ibid., 13, 64.

fixated on psychology.[75] But whatever claim he had on his enormous and grateful public's affection certainly rested on his suave blending of psychoanalysis and exhortation. His Freud, as it were, was to help God help man.

Liebman stopped short of integrating religion and psychology. He pleaded not for a marriage but for a partnership, for the most energetic and beneficent cooperation. This meant that he could reassure his readers: the invasion of Freudian analysis would not supplant religion in their hearts. "Under no circumstances," he insisted, "is the fear justified that psychiatry can ever take the place of religion or render the spiritual realm obsolete." While "the twain meet at many points, they differ profoundly both in goal and in substance."[76]

Liebman soothed his public on still another troubling issue. Was Freud not the most implacable adversary that religion, every religion including Judaism, has had to confront? Does Freud, the inveterate atheist, have anything to say to the devout? It was a problem, but Liebman solved it with characteristic ease. He acknowledged that Freud had had a "negative

75. To his fond widow, Joshua Loth Liebman was a true Renaissance man: "*Peace of Mind* is so heavily oriented—and quite properly so, of course—toward modern psychiatry that many have thought that, outside of religion, Dr. Liebman's entire interest lay in psychology. Psychology was, of course, one of his major interests—but only one. He earned his doctor's degree, as a matter of fact, in philosophy, his first love; he was deep-read in many fields of literature; he had more than a casual interest in music and art; he was no mere tyro in physics and mathematics; and he was always well versed in politics and national and international affairs. Among his friends he numbered scientists and senators, artists and novelists, university presidents, Nobel Prize winners and, of course, many spiritual leaders of all faiths." Fan Loth Liebman, "Preface," 6–7.

76. Liebman, *Peace of Mind* (1946), 180.

approach to religion," and that, along with "some of his disciples," he had been "biased." But, like some Christian divines eager to avail themselves of Freud, Liebman insisted that the Freudians' "antagonistic" point of view toward religion was not really central to psychoanalysis. It was, rather, "an accident of their personal biographies and does not in any way invalidate the spiritual helpfulness of their discoveries about human nature."[77] Indeed, fortunately Freud was far more religious than he knew: "Sigmund Freud, the founder of psychoanalysis, really had a spiritual purpose, even though he may not have been aware of it."[78] It is, then, perfectly safe for the religious reader to entrust himself to Freud—but only as directed by Liebman.

Liebman's prescription is straightforward and, as he might have said, heartwarming. His adroit chapter headings sum it up: "Conscience Doth Make Cowards"; "Love Thyself Properly"; "Love or Perish." On the surface, Liebman's counsel resembles Freud's letter: learn to know and to express yourself. But it is wholly alien to Freud's spirit. "Thou shalt not be

77. Ibid., 179. While Liebman does not spell out the biographical accidents he has in mind, the argument puts him into company with those, like the psychoanalyst Gregory Zilboorg and others, who find the roots of Freud's antireligious attitude in his early childhood. I quote Dr. Abraham Franzblau again: One of the "deeper" causes of Freud's atheism was "perhaps his reactions as a child of three to the frustrating episode when his old Catholic nurse, to whom he was devoted, was taken away from him. During the rest of his life, as he later discovered in his own analysis of himself, he unconsciously resented this deprivation. This may therefore have been a factor in his rejection of all that was associated in memory with his nurse—all orthodoxies and whatever else about religion he subsequently came to know." In Noveck, ed., *Judaism and Psychiatry,* 184. For other speculations along these reductionist lines, see above, pp. 57–58.

78. Ibid., 19.

afraid of thy hidden impulses" begins the list of Liebman's commandments—seven rather than ten—gently glancing at, but slyly subverting, the strenuous and unpleasant work the analysand must do on the couch. "Thou shalt transcend inner anxiety," Liebman goes on, apparently unaware that he is commending a goal that Freud showed to be an impossible fantasy. But Liebman's world is one in which all wounds can be healed, all troubles cured. Freud's astringent view of man as the ever-wishing, ever-conflict-ridden, ever-hating animal has vanished in a rosy haze of unlimited possibilities. Liebman had maintained in his concluding chapter that even his flexible religion was not identical with Freud's ideas. This is an understatement: Liebman's expansive, cheery self-help pamphlet is proof, on page after page, that even so yielding, so soft, so psychological a religiosity as Liebman's is, bluntly, the antithesis of Freud's science.

Unorthodox theologians—whether Jewish or Christian—infatuated, or at least impressed, with Freud were not alone in sketching a program for reconciliation. Just as a minority among believers has sought to rescue psychoanalysis for religion, a minority of psychoanalysts has sought to rescue religion for psychoanalysis. Ernest Jones, who spent most of his mature life among Jewish analysts, found them all to be wholehearted atheists: "It has never been my fortune to know a Jew possessing any religious belief, let alone an orthodox one."[79] He was

79. Ernest Jones, *Free Associations: Memories of a Psycho-Analyst* (1959), 210.

right enough: a look at the papers by Otto Rank, Theodor Reik, Sándor Ferenczi, or Karl Abraham on religious myth and ritual, on saints and holy days, shows that the first generation of psychoanalysts took the irreparable tension between science and religion simply for granted. Jones himself was no more disposed to traffic with religion, however liberal, than were those Jewish unbelievers. He long toyed with writing a "biology of religion." When Freud told Jones that he was thinking about some papers on religion, papers that would become *Totem and Taboo,* Jones urged him on enthusiastically: "The most exciting news in your letter was that you had determined to devote yourself to religious problems. Obviously that is the last and firmest stronghold of what may be called the anti-scientific, anti-rational, or anti-objective Weltanschauung, and no doubt it is there we may expect the most intense resistance, and the thick of the fight."[80]

But a later generation of psychoanalysts was no longer quite so categorical in its dismissal of all religion. One of the most prominent among the recruits of the mid-1920s, Erich Fromm, had come to psychoanalysis from an orthodox Jewish household and after studies with orthodox Jewish teachers and professors. His discovery of Marx, who would engage his lasting loyalties far more than Freud, gave his analytic writings, even in their most unexceptional "orthodox" Freudian phase, their recognizable flavor. Both Judaism, which he ostensibly abandoned in his twenties, and Marxism, which he never abandoned, strengthened his fervent—his critics would say, his messianic—

80. Jones to Freud, August 31, 1911. By permission of Sigmund Freud Copyrights, Wivenhoe.

ambition to construct a faith by which men could live. During the years in which he worked comfortably within the Freudian ambience, he published papers on religion wholly in the spirit of Theodor Reik's studies of ritual. But once he developed a sociological psychology of his own and grew increasingly skeptical about Freud the man and his work, his emphasis changed. In his immensely popular little book on the relation of religious beliefs to psychoanalysis, he situated analysis near the great founders of religions East and West. Their goal had been to aid the "unfolding" of mankind's "powers of love and reason." As Fromm saw it, "psychoanalysis, far from being a threat to this aim, can on the contrary contribute a great deal to its realization."[81] Fundamentally, psychoanalysis is a religious quest: "There is no one without a religious need, a need to have a frame of orientation and an object of devotion."[82] Employing rhetoric closely resembling Pfister's, he defined psychoanalysis as the cure of souls.

This was indeed poaching on Pfister's territory: as one might expect, Fromm found the key to this cure in Eros. "*Analytic therapy is essentially an attempt to help the patient gain or regain his capacity for love.*"[83] There is, as we have seen, some warrant in Freud's writings for singling out love as the privileged remedy for mental malaise and the supreme sign of recovery. But Freud's dry and bracingly pessimistic tone sharply differs from Fromm's: it is less exalted, less sentimental, closer to reality. Freud, we know, was willing to think of love as the ground of

81. Fromm, *Psychoanalysis and Religion* (1950), 99.
82. Ibid., 25.
83. Ibid., 87. Italics in the original.

human experience, he told Pfister, if hatred were added to the picture. This is not to say that Fromm left the Freudian camp entirely. The help that the analyst extends to his patient consists in strengthening his capacity for criticism: if one cannot make valid statements about God, one can "make such statements about the negative, about idols." Is it "not time," Fromm pointedly asks, "to cease to argue about God and instead to unite in the unmasking of contemporary forms of idolatry?" The modern idols crying out for exposure are "the deification of the state and of power in authoritarian countries and the deification of the machine and of success in our own culture."[84] This praise of criticism, concrete political implications apart, was good psychoanalytic talk.

But then it was a matter of indifference to Fromm whether people are "religionists" or not. The supreme need is to unite "in firm negation of idolatry" and in the search for a "common faith in this negation."[85] Fromm was not a theist. What he preached is "humility" and "brotherly love."[86] This pacific eclecticism, this indifference to what religion one professes as long as it is not idolatrous, as long as one cares about the spirit rather than the words or the institutions, would have struck Freud as a sad retreat from the scientific spirit.

Fromm's prescription was quite general, a matter of attitudes rather than dogma. But a few of his colleagues, notably the British psychoanalyst Marjorie Brierley, found a place in psychoanalytic thinking not just for the religious spirit but for the

84. Ibid., 118–19.
85. Ibid., 119.
86. Ibid.

Christian spirit. In her discussion of what she calls "integrative living"—in short, mental health, a subject that Freud, convinced that all humans are a little neurotic, on the whole avoided—Brierley found in Christianity "a method of integration." Contradicting most other cultural commentators, she was confident that its "rapid demise" is far from probable. It might even survive side by side with the human sciences because the "conviction of Christians that their religion will endure is not merely 'wish-fulfilling,' but psychologically justifiable."[87]

"Psychologically" justifiable: Brierley's adverb is revealing. To her mind, the Christian religion has access to psychological truths, and hence aptly serves human needs. "The desire to worship and adore is not a minor aberration but one of the strongest human passions." She conceded that modern religion may be "inherently unstable," for even tolerant Protestants tend to "perpetuate civil war within the personality." She conceded, too, as R. S. Lee had before her, that the antireligious animus of the scientific community is well founded. Yet, like William James, Brierley criticized the rationalists for "dealing only with the superficial manifestations of profound needs which religion had at least appeased." She even saw some force in the argument that "the modern chaos of human values" is due to "the breakdown of religion." Certainly the conservative remedy, "return to obsolete dogma and ritual," is too primitive. But what mankind needs to "discover is how to live without the comfort of illusion." Freud, of course, had made this very aspiration

87. Brierley, *Trends in Psycho-Analysis* (1951), 87, 118–19.

the centerpiece of his program for human enlightenment through psychoanalysis. But Brierley's definition of illusion differed markedly from Freud's clear-cut atheistic definition; her heart was in religion, more precisely in a reasonable Christianity, whatever its demonstrable shortcomings. She was cheered to see fresh, heartening interpretations of her faith springing up all around her. "Christianity may be challenged and on the defensive, but it is also challenging and on the offensive."[88] Which was just what gave Freud cause for grim foreboding.

Brierley had been pleased to note, as had Fromm, that even some Roman Catholic theologians were beginning to engage in a dialogue with psychoanalysis. Pope Pius XII expressly condemned psychoanalysis as a "pansexualist method" that debases ethics and corrodes the soul.[89] But other Catholics, as we have seen, adopted a far more forgiving posture. Among the most interesting of these was the psychoanalyst Gregory Zilboorg, a facile and prolific essayist who had given religion a good press for some years before his conversion to Catholicism. Zilboorg's arguments are all familiar, if brought forward in his writings with exceptional fluency. While Freud himself, Zilboorg noted, would have rebuffed any attempt to identify his ideas with those of Christian theologians, in fact, when attentively read, St. Thomas Aquinas on the soul or many other devout authors on love disclose fundamental affinities between

88. Ibid., 18, 174–75, 100, 155, 204.
89. "Die sittlichen Grenzen der ärztlichen Forschungs- und Behandlungsmethoden," a speech of September 14, 1952; selections in Johannes Cremerius, ed., *Die Rezeption der Psychoanalyse in der Soziologie, Psychologie und Theologie im deutschsprachigen Raum bis 1940* (1981), 296.

Christian and psychoanalytic doctrine. Even the "concept of
original sin or of the original fall of man," Zilboorg maintains,
"finds its empirical counterpart in the findings of psychoanalysis."⁹⁰ He thought it a matter of real regret that Freud shut
his eyes to these truths. This was "scientism, not scientific."
To Zilboorg, Freud was caught in a fascinating contradiction:
he "stood in his own way, so to speak."⁹¹ As the psychologist
who had made pioneering discoveries about the nature of love
and of guilt, he had been beautifully placed to appreciate the
work that religion does for the individual and for culture.
Instead he had treated it with contempt. Freud was a great
man, Zilboorg had no doubt, but from a religious perspective,
he must be pronounced a tragic failure.

All this peacemaking, all this putting Freud in his place,
whether from the theologian's or the psychoanalyst's vantage
point, has amounted to very little. Freud, at any rate, was not
disposed to be grateful to the best-intentioned of ecumenical
efforts. His critique of the moral-theological speculations in
which the eminent American neurologist James Jackson Putnam liked to indulge exhibits this attitude to perfection. Putnam had become a recruit to psychoanalysis late in life, and
Freud valued him, the famous Harvard professor, no less for

90. Zilboorg, "Psyche, Soul and Religion," last chapter of *Mind, Medicine
and Man* (1943), reprinted in *Psychoanalysis and Religion* (1967), 45.
91. Zilboorg, "Scientific Psychopathology and Religious Issues" (1953),
in ibid., 105.

his own sake than for the prestige he might bring to Freud's young and embattled movement. In 1915, Putnam published *Human Motives,* in which he bravely mixed psychology and ethics, psychoanalysis and theology, and reasoned that God must exist because humans can conceive of His being. Freud frankly demurred: "I cannot find the transition from the ps. reality of our perfections to their actual existence," he told Putnam. He added, a little mischievously, "I am not afraid at all of the Almighty"; if he and God should ever happen to meet, he, Freud, would reproach God for not endowing him with better intellectual equipment.[92] That was candid enough, but two days later, writing to his confidant Sándor Ferenczi, Freud addressed the deeper reason for his discontent with *Human Motives.* If the book had not been intended as a popularization, "I would say, it is poor. Worthy as always, loyal, too," but "filled with the religious sense which I am irresistibly inclined to reject."[93]

For Freud, then, the common ground that some had discovered between psychoanalysis and faith was a swampy, treacherous bog in which both must sink. How swampy emerges from a glance at *Psychoanalysis and Religious Experience* by W. W. Meissner, whom I have mentioned before. Meissner wrestles with, among other topics, Freud's correspondence with Pfister.

92. Freud to Putnam, July 8, 1915. My translation from the original German text in Nathan G. Hale, Jr., ed., *James Jackson Putnam and Psychoanalysis: Letters between Putnam and Sigmund Freud, Ernest Jones, William James, Sándor Ferenczi and Morton Prince, 1877–1917* (1971), 376.

93. Freud to Ferenczi, July 10, 1915. Freud-Ferenczi Correspondence, Freud Collection, LC.

Being both a Jesuit and a psychoanalyst, he writes as an insider in the two mutually hostile worlds he hopes in some way to reconcile. But he is compelled to concede that even the most "nuanced and sophisticated" psychoanalysis must remain distinct and separate from religion: "In a sense, theology takes up where psychoanalysis leaves off." They may become neighbors but not partners. All one can hope for is "mutual reinforcement and dialogue."[94] The earnest, energetic efforts at reconciliation that had gone before Meissner reached this rather despairing conclusion, efforts that had begun in 1908 with Pfister, have proved to be protracted negotiations that led nowhere, ending only in a declaration of failure.

The failure would doubtless have amused Freud, but it would not have surprised him. It was inevitable, in fact predictable. The most ingenious scholarship or most embracing pacifism could not, and should not, erase the enmity between science and theology, psychoanalysis and religion. Near the end of his life, Freud reiterated this conviction once more in a letter to Charles Singer, the distinguished historian of science. Singer had been troubled by Freud's forthcoming *Moses and Monotheism,* which he feared would be an attack on the Jewish religion. It is "an attack on religion," Freud replied, "only in so far as, after all, every scientific investigation of a religious belief has unbelief as its presupposition."[95] Nothing could be more lapidary, or more conclusive, than this. Freud, we know, said that it had had to be a godless Jew who fathered psychoanalysis.

94. Meissner, *Psychoanalysis and Religious Experience* (1984), vii, 19, 240.
95. Freud to Singer, October 31, 1938. *Briefe,* 469.

The first part of that claim, the godlessness, has, I think, now been firmly established. But a Jew? That question still awaits an answer.

❀ THREE

The Question of a Jewish Science:

"A Title of Honor"

T o label psychoanalysis a "Jewish science" is to accept some unwelcome company. Its partisans have formed an incongruous alliance that embraces Jews eager to claim Freud and grudging gentiles just as eager to disparage him. On the one side one finds A. A. Roback, a Yiddishist and psychologist, asking in the late 1920s, "Is psychoanalysis a Jewish movement?" and pleased to answer in the affirmative.[1] On the other side there is William McDougall, that prolific and prestigious social psychologist: "The famous theory of Freud," he wrote in 1921, "is a theory of the development and working of the mind which was evolved by a Jew who has studied chiefly Jewish patients; and it seems to appeal very strongly to Jews; many, perhaps the majority of those physicians who accept it as a new gospel, a new revelation, are Jews." Here, I may interpolate, are those facile, it seems inescapable, theological metaphors again. "It looks as though his theory," McDougall concludes, "which to me and to most men of my sort seems to be strange, bizarre and fantastic, may be approximately true of the Jewish

1. Roback, *Jewish Influences in Modern Thought* (1929), 160.

race."[2] He is paraphrasing Jung, but expressly making Jung's observation his own.

Nevertheless, the epithet "Jewish science" enjoys the endorsement of the highest possible authority: Anna Freud. In 1977, she concluded the inaugural lecture she had written for the Sigmund Freud Chair at the Hebrew University in Jerusalem on that most provocative note: psychoanalysis "has been criticized for its methods being imprecise, its findings not open to proof by experiment, for being unscientific, even for being a 'Jewish science.' However the other derogatory comments may be evaluated, it is, I believe, the last-mentioned connotation which, under present circumstances, can serve as a title of honor."[3] In view of Anna Freud's well-known reluctance to

2. McDougall, *Is America Safe for Democracy?* (1921), 127. I should note that McDougall explicitly rejected the anti-Semitic racial theories then current (see ibid., 27–33) and that he professed to value Freud highly. In a set of lectures devoted to a critique of psychoanalysis that he delivered at the University of London in 1935, McDougall took the trouble to declare, "In order that there may be no mistake about my attitude to Professor Freud, I add that in my judgment he is a great man, both morally and intellectually; I esteem and admire him greatly." If, he observes, "my criticism is ruthless, it is nevertheless entirely friendly; and it aspires to be constructive. If from among all the rival systems of psychology I have singled out as the object of my critical attack the system of Freud, it is not that I regard his views as more in need of criticism than any other, it is rather because I hold Freud's system to be the most deserving of honest criticism." *Psycho-Analysis and Social Psychology* (1936), 17*n*, vi. The reader may be forgiven if he mutters something like, With such friends Freud needs no enemies.

3. Anna Freud, Inaugural Lecture (read in Jerusalem in August 1977 by Arthur F. Valenstein). *Int. Jl. of Psycho-Anal.*, LIX (1978), 148. The paragraph seems to have stirred the audience deeply. As one participant, Paul Schwaber, wrote, "People hesitated, turned, wondered: a Jewish science! It came from nowhere in the speech. Yet under the circumstances of the Hebrew University—a title of honor. Maintaining her reserve, but emphatically at the climax, Anna Freud faced down the old issue, unexpectedly, transvaluing

depart from her father's views, it is an affirmation we overlook at our own risk.

But Anna Freud's intentions are not immediately obvious. Her statement draws its meaning from recent history; it was, after all, "under present circumstances" that she thought psychoanalysis should take this term of opprobrium and wear it proudly as a badge of honor. She was not, then, characterizing the origins of psychoanalysis. Has psychoanalysis somehow *become* Jewish with the passage of time? Has the pressure of loyalty, the memory of Hitler's victims, compelled the survivors to proclaim its essential Jewishness? Such questions point to the murky atmosphere in which the debate has been carried on for decades, but they do not clear it up. As we have just seen, admirers of Freud and detractors alike did not wait for the horrors of the 1930s and 1940s to bestow the name of Jewish on psychoanalysis. Indeed, Jews were by no means passive in this enterprise. In the manner of Pfister trying to make Freud into a Christian, Jews tried to enlist him in their own ranks. In 1931, congratulating Freud on his seventy-fifth birthday, David Feuchtwang, then chief rabbi of Vienna, pointedly addressed his good wishes to "the great—by no means least, Jewish—researcher and scholar and man. Perhaps the last roots and germs of your intellectual construction are to be sought in

---

values. The very quality of unencumbered statement suggests that the tension has not been resolved but dealt with differently. Nonetheless, with proximate distance still, she bespoke a changed attitude. An historical moment." "Title of Honor: The Psychoanalytic Congress in Jerusalem," *Midstream,* XXIV (March 1978), 32.

the Jewish terrestrial realm—perhaps. The author of *The Future of an Illusion* is closer to me than he thinks."[4]

Anna Freud's father did his strenuous best not to think so; all his life he labored to frustrate such an identification. Speaking of Jung to Karl Abraham in 1908, Freud commented, "Only his appearance has saved psychoanalysis from becoming a Jewish national concern."[5] His goal in cultivating the gentile psychiatrists in Zurich had been, he told Ferenczi four years later, "to amalgamate Jews and goyim in the service of Psa."[6] The most emotional scene he ever made in public grew from this anxious effort. At the second international congress of psychoanalysts meeting at Nürnberg in March 1910, the newly formed international association chose Jung as its president and Jung's relative Riklin as its secretary. This slap at his Viennese followers had been Freud's idea. But obedient and subservient as they usually showed themselves, this time they were infuriated, appalled. In a rare show of independence, they convoked a private protest meeting to take counsel. Freud got wind of the conclave, walked in on it, and in an excited speech pleaded with them to grasp the inconvenient truth that the Swiss, the gentiles, would rescue them from their isolation and guarantee the future of their movement. One eyewitness, Wilhelm Stekel, in whose hotel room this drama unfolded, recalled that Freud was so overwrought that he had tears running down his

4. David Feuchtwang to Freud, April 7, 1931. Freud Museum, London.

5. Freud to Abraham, May 3, 1908. *Freud-Abraham*, 47 (34).

6. Freud to Ferenczi, July 28, 1912. Freud-Ferenczi Correspondence, Freud Collection, LC.

cheeks.[7] Stekel is not a reliable witness, but tears or not, Freud did not want psychoanalysis to be—or to be known as—a Jewish science.

Freud had no difficulty with the notion that there are palpable differences between Jews and "aryans." He was even willing to speak of "racial" differences, as people did so easily in those innocent days. In the spring of 1908, Freud urged Karl Abraham, who had worked with Jung for some years and did not trust him, to be tolerant of the Swiss and to remember that it was easier for him, as a Jew, than for Jung, "as a Christian and the son of a pastor," to overcome his resistances to Freudian ideas. He described himself as particularly close to Abraham because of their "racial kinship—*Rassenverwandtschaft*," and soon after added: "May I say that it is kindred Jewish traits that attract me in you?"[8] During the years that his friendship with Jung was going sour and his relations to his gentile supporters in Zurich were strained and uncertain, he asserted the existence of such racial kinship freely. But he insisted at the same time that "there should be no distinct aryan or Jewish science." If the results reached by a Jewish and a gentile scientist differ, there must be something wrong somewhere.[9] For Freud, science is color-blind, indifferent to na-

7. See Stekel, *The Autobiography of Wilhelm Stekel: The Life Story of a Pioneer Psychoanalyst,* ed. Emil A. Gutheil (1950), 128. For a less melodramatic, and it would seem more accurate, account, see Fritz Wittels, *Sigmund Freud: The Man, His Personality and His School* (1924; tr. Eden and Cedar Paul, 1924), 139–40.

8. Freud to Abraham, May 3, July 23, 1908. *Freud-Abraham,* 47, 57 (34, 46).

9. Freud to Ferenczi, June 8, 1913. Freud-Ferenczi Correspondence, Freud Collection, LC.

tional, ethnic, racial qualities—and psychoanalysis is a science. Hence he could never have accepted the description of psychoanalysis as a Jewish science, on intellectual as much as on political grounds. But many have preferred the daughter's to the father's conclusion, and kept the issue open.

The issue is electric with emotion; and the investment in affirming, or in denying, the Jewishness of psychoanalysis is heavy in the extreme. It is not that Freud ever concealed, or prevaricated about, his Jewish origins and allegiances. He liked to speak of them with pride and a certain truculent tone, and not just to his fellow-Jews. He called himself, we know, a shabby old Israelite; he called himself an "old Semite."[10] Thanking the Hebrew University in Jerusalem for its greetings to him on his eightieth birthday, he confessed himself, once again, "one of yours."[11] Some years before, he had told a correspondent who had inquired about his relations to Judaism, "I can say that I am as remote from the Jewish religion as from all others; that is to say, they are highly significant to me as a subject of scientific interest; emotionally I am not involved in them. On the other hand, I have always had a strong feeling of solidarity with my people and have also fostered it in my children. We have all remained in the Jewish confession."[12]

Freud gave expression to this solidarity in moments sober

10. Freud to Ernst Kris, June 7, 1931 (I owe this letter to Dr. Anna K. Wolff).

11. Freud to Hebrew University, Jerusalem, May 1936. Freud Collection, B4, LC.

12. Freud to "Sehr geehrter Herr," January 27, 1925. Dictated to and typed by, Anna Freud. By permission of Sigmund Freud Copyrights, Wivenhoe.

and playful alike. In early October 1913, as he was making ready to resume his psychoanalytic practice in Vienna after his long, refreshing summer holiday, Max Eitingon sent him the "old Jewish New Year's greeting, *l'shanah tovah*," with which, Eitingon recalled, Freud had once, "years ago, closed one of our congresses."[13] And Freud's letters to correspondents in Palestine testify to his marked interest in their enterprise. "Zionism," he recalled in 1930, "awakened my strongest sympathies, which are still faithfully attached to it today."[14] Five years later, he sent a letter to L. Jaffe in Jerusalem to help celebrate the fifteenth anniversary of Keren Hajessod, a foundation for the resettlement of Jews in Palestine: "I want to assure you that I know full well how powerfully and beneficently effective an instrument this foundation has become for our people in the endeavor to found a new home in the old fatherland." Keren Hajessod was, he noted in his characteristic defiant tone, "a sign of our invincible will to live which has so far successfully braved two thousand years of burdensome oppression! Our youth will continue to carry on the fight."[15]

That was in private, but Freud never hesitated to make these feelings public: in his short self-portrait, published in 1925, he said plainly that his ancestors had been Jewish and that he, too, had remained a Jew.[16] In the unsettled atmosphere of

13. Eitingon to Freud, October 1 (1913). By permission of Sigmund Freud Copyrights, Wivenhoe.

14. Freud to J. Dwossis, Jerusalem, December 15, 1930. Typed transcription, Freud Museum, London.

15. Freud to L. Jaffe, June 20, 1935. Typed transcription, ibid.

16. "Selbstdarstellung," *GW* XIV, 34 / "Autobiographical Study," *SE* XX, 7.

postwar Europe, with racial political anti-Semitism a fright-
ening and growing menace, this was a conscious, deliberate
declaration of allegiance, not lacking civic courage. Freud was
aware that to be, and remain, a Jew was a hard lot. But the
illusory escape route of baptism, whether taken from conviction
or policy, one that many of his contemporaries like Alfred Adler
would follow, struck him as contemptible.

Unequivocal as it was, Freud's identification with Judaism
was aggressively secular. He had acquired this secularism early,
at home. Nor had his beloved teacher and paternal friend Samuel Hammerschlag, in charge of religious instruction at Freud's
Gymnasium, done much if anything to repair this domestic
neglect. Hammerschlag was far more interested in ethics than
in theology, let alone the Hebrew language.[17] In later years,
Freud repeatedly regretted that he was unfortunately not master
of the "holy language."[18] It was not that he had repressed his

17. Freud's situation seems to have been fairly typical. As one Jewish
commentator lamented in the latter part of the nineteenth century, speaking
of Austria: "True, the Jewish father of our time provides with praiseworthy
zeal for the general education of his son, but he has precious little concern
for his Jewish education. The Jewish father, all too worried about the career
of his son, is of the opinion that even the two to three hours a week devoted
to lessons in the Hebrew language and the Bible could be devoted and
employed far more advantageously to other studies." I. Singer, *Presse und
Judentum* (2d ed., 1882), 14, quoted in Johannes Barta, *Jüdische Familienerziehung: Das jüdische Erziehungswesen im 19. und 20. Jahrhundert* (1974), 76.

18. For one instance among several, see "Vorrede zur hebräischen Ausgabe" of *Totem and Taboo* (written 1930, published 1934), *GW* XIV, 569 /
Preface to the Hebrew translation of *Totem and Taboo*, *SE* XIII, xv. For another:
"Unfortunately I cannot read Hebrew." Freud to J. Dwossis, December 11,
1938. Typed transcription, Freud Museum, London.

Hebrew; he had never really known it well. His father, Jacob Freud, who did know Hebrew, was no more religious for all that. He had married his third wife, Amalia Nathansohn, who was to become Freud's mother, in a Reform ceremony and had, in the course of years, shed virtually all traces of religious observance. He continued to celebrate Passover and to read the Bible—in Hebrew—but that was all. He had his son circumcised, yet there is no evidence that Freud had even a trace of religious instruction at home, or a Bar Mitzvah. "My father," Freud remembered in old age, "spoke the sacred language as well as German or better. He let me grow up in complete ignorance of everything that concerned Judaism." It was only as a mature man, he added, that he had taken this neglect in bad part. "But I had already felt as a Jew earlier—under the impact of German anti-Semitism, whose more recent outbreak occurred during my university days."[19] But if Freud came to regret the ignorance in which his father had left him about Judaism, that was not because he felt emotionally starved for religious beliefs, festivals, or ceremonies.

Nor did Freud grant them entry to his own household. The Freuds studiously ignored even such companionable, domestic Jewish holidays as Passover. "Our festivals," his son Martin recalled, "were Christmas, with presents under a candle-lit tree, and Easter, with gaily painted Easter eggs. I had never been in a synagogue, nor to my knowledge had my brother or sisters."[20] During his engagement, Freud firmly insisted that

19. Freud to J. Dwossis, Jerusalem, December 15, 1930. Typed transcription, Freud Museum, London.
20. Martin Freud, "Who was Freud?" Josef Fraenkel, ed., *The Jews of Austria: Essays on their Life, History and Destruction* (1967), 203.

his fiancée give up her cherished orthodox beliefs and practices. But his domestic authoritarianism was selective: when his son Ernst became active in the Austrian Zionist movement after the First World War, Freud did not object. It is a measure, though, of the innocence about Judaism in which he and his children lived that his son Martin did not know the most rudimentary rules of conduct in a synagogue. When he got married, he recounts, he went through the religious ceremony that the law of the land required. Dressed up in top hat and tails, he showed his respect to the holy place he was entering by taking off his hat. When the escort on his left firmly placed his hat back on his head, he took it as a joke and promptly took it off again. It was only when the escort on his right repeated the other escort's gesture, and when he saw the indignant looks on the faces of the assembled wedding guests that the difference between Jewish holy places and others dawned on Martin Freud.[21]

Freud was glad to delineate the contours of his Jewishness to anyone curious enough to inquire. "I adhere to the Jewish religion as little as to any other," he wrote in 1929.[22] In the following year, he described himself, in the preface to the Hebrew translation of *Totem and Taboo,* as "wholly estranged from the religion of his fathers—as from every other." But he insisted at the same time that he had "never denied his affiliation with his people."[23] He had often said the same thing in his

21. See ibid., 203–04.
22. Freud to Isaac Landman, August 1, 1929. Typed transcription, Freud Collection, B3, LC.
23. "Vorrede zur hebräischen Ausgabe," *GW* XIV, 569 / Preface to the Hebrew translation of *Totem and Taboo, SE* XIII, xv.

letters. "Though long since estranged from the religion of my forefathers," he wrote in 1926 to an Italian professor, Enrico Morselli, who had recently published a critical study of psychoanalysis, "I have never given up the feeling of solidarity with my people."[24] He characterized himself once more, succinctly but accurately, to a pious American physician who had told Freud of a religious vision and invited him to study such experiences that he, too, might find God. Politely but firmly, Freud replied that God had not done that much for him and had sent him no inner voices; hence he was likely to remain what he had been, "an infidel Jew."[25]

Freud's Jewish identity, then, is not in question. What *is* in question is just what share that identity could have had in the making of psychoanalysis. "I do not know if you are right in your judgment," Freud wrote to Morselli in 1926, "which wants to see psychoanalysis as a direct product of the Jewish spirit, but if it were so, I would not feel ashamed."[26] But just what is the Jewish spirit? How may one sensibly speak of a Jewish quality in—or absence from—psychoanalysis? It is important, but difficult, to be precise. To work toward that precision I propose to discriminate four meanings in that quality: the professional, the intellectual, the tribal, and the sociological.

24. Freud to Enrico Morselli, February 18, 1926. *Briefe,* 380.
25. "A Religious Experience" (1928), *SE* XXI, 170. In English in the original.
26. Freud to Morselli, February 18, 1926. *Briefe,* 380.

Psychoanalysis might be said to show certain Jewish characteristics if it were principally Jewish in its materials—in its patients, or in such documentation as the slips or the jokes Freud enlisted in evidence. The results are thin. In the absence of a full repertory of Freud's analysands, we are reduced to conjectures and inferences. Certainly a disproportionate number especially among his early patients, as Jung had observed, were Jews. So was the founding patient of psychoanalysis, Josef Breuer's famous Anna O. But these proportions drastically shifted as Freud's practice expanded. While among his published patients, Dora, the Rat Man, and Little Hans were Jewish, the Wolf-Man and Schreber, one a Russian aristocrat and the other a German judge, were not. Moreover, while the American physicians who streamed to his couch in the 1920s were for the most part Jews, his best-known later patients were gentiles: the Dutch physician Jeanne Lampl de Groot, the French princess Marie Bonaparte, the American poet Hilda Doolittle, the cluster of English analysands, James and Alix Strachey, Joan Riviere, and others. They all, Jew or gentile, taught Freud the same lessons about the workings of the mind. The unconscious, the libido, acts of repression and sublimation are, as Freud thought them to be, universal. None of them obeys specifically Jewish imperatives.

Freud's collection of faulty actions—slips of tongue or pen, forgetting of names, dates, or poems—yields a harvest even slighter. The "profound Jewish stories" he cherished, began to collect in the late 1890s,[27] and scattered through his book on

27. See Freud to Fliess, June 22, 1897. *Freud-Fliess*, 271 (254).

the relation of jokes to the unconscious seem intriguing at first. With their mixture of self-denigration and self-respect, submissiveness and rebelliousness, their way of establishing intimacy in a hostile world, they strongly appealed to Freud. But far from providing evidence for the Jewish qualities in Freud's psychoanalytic thought, these jokes rather attest to its universality. It was not what made them Jewish, but what made the joking Jews human that engaged Freud's attention. Telling one of these jokes in his book, he comments that only its superficial details are Jewish; "its core is general-human."[28] It was the core that mattered.

The effort to provide Freud with a Jewish intellectual ancestry is no more productive than the search for his Jewishness in his patients or his jokes. His principal debts, which he recounted often and exhibited for all to see, were to German and English culture: to German and English poets no less than German and English scientists—to Goethe and Shakespeare, Brücke and Darwin. The most cursory glance at one of Freud's pages reveals a master of the German language at work, a stylist who has absorbed the precision, wit, and felicity of Lessing and Heine and Wilhelm Busch. In 1907, replying to a questionnaire about ten "good books" sent around by his publisher Hugo Heller, he chose to report on his favorites, on comfortable literary companions rather than the imperishable classics or the scientific treatises that had most influenced him. Freud's list is remarkable for its catholicity; it includes writers from seven countries: Mark Twain and Lord Macaulay, Anatole France and

28. *Der Witz und seine Beziehung zum Unbewussten* (1905), *GW* VI, 51 / *Jokes and their Relation to the Unconscious*, *SE* VI, 49.

Emile Zola, Dmitri Merezhkovski and Gottfried Keller and Conrad Ferdinand Meyer. There is only one Jew in Freud's catalogue of ten: the classical philologist Theodor Gomperz with his history of Greek thought, a cultivated scholar and essayist who was wholly secular, wholly identified with the values of the European Enlightenment—in short, a Jew very much like Freud himself.[29]

In light of this copious record, it takes a certain audacity to discover an impact of the Jewish mystics on Freud, and it is not surprising that there have been few serious attempts to construct such a pedigree. In 1929, A. A. Roback called Freud "The *Chassid* in the history of modern psychology." He meant to bestow the highest possible praise on Freud by pointing to his presumed mystical leanings; this just two years after Freud had published *The Future of an Illusion.* The rationalist message of that "brochure" did not deter Roback. "Freud's method," as he saw it, is "strongly reminiscent of the *symbolism* which underlies the Cabbalistic philosophy."[30] Three decades later, in a study much criticized but much quoted, David Bakan expanded Roback's observation into a book, offering no more persuasive evidence than Roback had been able to muster. Bakan's claim that the spirit of the Cabbala is alive in Freud contradicts everything we know of Freud's mind: his reading, his style of scientific inquiry, his whole way of thinking.[31] The

29. See "Contribution to a Questionnaire on Reading" (1907), *SE* IX, 245–47.
30. Roback, *Jewish Influences in Modern Thought,* 160–61.
31. Bakan, *Sigmund Freud and the Jewish Mystical Tradition* (1958). For a brief but to my mind decisive criticism, see Marthe Robert, *From Oedipus to Moses: Freud's Jewish Identity* (1974; tr. Ralph Manheim, 1976), 171–72. Freud did once refer to his "Jewish mysticism," in a letter to Jung, confessing

eminent French-Jewish psychiatrist Henri Baruk had a point when he rose during a scholarly colloquy in Paris in the 1960s to denounce, indignantly, "the notion of those who, uninformed, tell us that Freud was a Jewish mystic or a rabbi. The exact opposite is true." Baruk argued, rather, in accord with the best evidence, that psychoanalysis is really a "modern neopaganism."[32] It is no accident that Freud, always ready to acknowledge his sources, never so much as alludes to the ancestors that Roback and Bakan invented for him. Quite the contrary: writing to Karl Abraham about what he thought the special gift of Jews for psychoanalysis, Freud explained it by the fact that Jews *lack* the mystical element.[33] A number of years later, he reiterated this disclaimer to Hans Ehrenwald in acknowledging a copy of Ehrenwald's book, *Über den sogenannten jüdischen Geist*: "Several years ago I began to pose the question to myself how the Jews had acquired the character peculiar to them." He confessed that he "had not got very far," but had been driven to conclude that it had been "the first, so to speak embryonic experience of the people," the impact of Moses and the exodus from Egypt, that had stamped Jews through the centuries. "In the first place there is the this-worldliness of the

his superstition about fatal numbers. Freud to Jung, April 16, 1909. *Freud-Jung*, 242–43 (218–20).

32. Baruk, "La signification de la psychanalyse et le Judaïsme," *Revue d'Histoire de la Médecine Hébraïque*, XIX (1966), 58.

33. See Freud to Abraham, July 20, 1908. *Freud-Abraham*, 56 (46). For his part, Abraham thought that psychoanalysis showed, if not precisely mystical, at least talmudic qualities. "After all," he told Freud, "the talmudic way of thinking cannot suddenly have disappeared from us." Looking at Freud's book on jokes, he found himself fascinated by a passage in which the intellectual style, confrontation and construction, was "wholly talmudic." Abraham to Freud, May 11, 1908. Ibid., 48–49 (36). This, I think, was not Freud's considered opinion.

view of life and the overcoming of magical thinking, and the rejection of mysticism."[34] It was precisely by rejecting mysticism, rather than by smuggling it in, that Freud had made his science.

In drastic contrast, the other two ways that Jewishness might have made its contribution to psychoanalysis, the tribal and the sociological, are far more promising. Freud, for one, embraced both. He believed his Jewishness to be an indefinable, elusive element at work within him. When the English psychoanalyst M. D. Eder, one of his earliest if not always most consistent followers, died in 1936, Freud mournfully dwelt on that mystery: "I can easily imagine how he, too, must have suffered under the bitterness of these times," he wrote to a common friend. "We were both Jews and knew of each other that we carried that miraculous thing in common, which—

34. Freud to Ehrenwald, December 14, 1937. Typed transcription, Freud Museum, London. Early in 1930, acknowledging receipt of Roback's *Jewish Influences in Modern Thought,* Freud demurred from Roback's coronation of him as one of the "intellectual sovereigns" Judaism had produced, including Bergson and Einstein, and declared himself uneasy with Roback's characterizations of him: "In some of your claims I do not recognize myself (for example, no one has yet reproached me with *mystical leanings* . . .)." He added for good measure: "It will interest you to hear that my father actually did spring from a chassidic milieu. He was forty-one years old when I was born and estranged from his domestic connections for almost twenty years. I was brought up in so un-Jewish a fashion that today I am not even in a position to read your dedication, obviously written in the Jewish script. In later years I have often regretted this piece of my ignorance." But he could not be seriously offended with Roback; his "manly championship of our people" compelled Freud to a certain admiration. Freud to Roback, February 20, 1930. Italicized words in English in the original. *Briefe,* 412.

inaccessible to any analysis so far—makes the Jew."[35] This miraculous thing had been on his mind for some years. In 1926, acknowledging the greetings of his brethren at B'nai B'rith on his seventieth birthday, he described himself, as he had so often before, as an "unbeliever" who had been "brought up without religion" though not without "respect for the demands, called 'ethical,' of human culture." He deprecated any Jewish national pride, which he thought an unjust, downright pernicious attitude. "But enough else remained to make the attraction of Judaism and of Jews so irresistible, many dark emotional powers—*Gefühlsmächte*—all the mightier the less they allow themselves to be grasped in words, as well as the clear consciousness of inner identity, the secrecy of the same mental construction."[36] Freud might insist on his "clear consciousness" of his Jewish identity, but these shadowy intimations obscure more than they clarify. As he was well aware, they scarcely constitute rational analysis.

I would suggest that Freud's undefined sense of Jewishness represents a special case of his obstinate belief in the inheritance of acquired characteristics. In *Totem and Taboo* he had argued that all mankind must forever labor under the primal crime, the killing and eating of the father, which constituted the founding act of civilization. In the same way, he believed, the Jews have borne through the centuries the burden of killing Moses and of the harsh, obsessive, self-punishing religion they developed after committing that murder. Freud saw his Jewishness as somehow part of his phylogenetic endowment. In

35. Freud to Barbara Low, April 19, 1936, in English. Ibid., 443.
36. Freud to the members of B'nai B'rith (May 6, 1926). Ibid., 381.

1922, he mused to Ferenczi about "strange secret longings" rising up within him, "perhaps from the heritage of my ancestors—for the Orient and the Mediterranean and a life of quite another kind: wishes from late childhood ill-adapted to reality."[37] His passion for antiquities, those plaques and statuettes Freud collected so assiduously through the years, was richly overdetermined. But certainly one reason informing what he called his "partiality for the prehistoric" was their power to remind him of a world he would never visit yet to which he thought he secretly belonged. This is what Freud wanted to convey in his preface to the Hebrew translation of *Totem and Taboo*: he had given up a great deal he might have in common with other Jews, yet what remained of his Jewishness was "still a great deal, probably the main thing." It was only that he could not express "this essence" in words, at least not for the present. "Surely it will some day be accessible to scientific insight."[38] This was the Jew as psychoanalyst: he treated his feeling of Jewish identity as akin to Romain Rolland's oceanic feeling, as a psychological phenomenon open in principle to investigation, but still enigmatic, still beyond science.

Freud's misty intimations fail to resolve the issue of just how and what his mysterious "racial" heritage had contributed to the making of psychoanalysis. I have quoted his hints to his most dependable Jewish followers that Jews are exceptionally equipped to do psychoanalysis. But he made very little of the notorious boast that the Jews, being the people of the book,

37. Freud to Ferenczi, March 30, 1922. Freud-Ferenczi Correspondence, Freud Collection, LC.
38. "Vorrede," *GW* XIV, 569 / Preface, *SE* XIII, xv.

are, as it were, chosen for the sort of intellectual pursuit that Freud had undertaken.[39] Others felt far freer than he did to define the undefinable. We may dismiss as frivolous the observation that psychoanalysis is typically Jewish because in the clinical hour the analyst answers a question with a question. More serious was the argument of A. A. Roback, who was, he said, "disposed to look for the actual causes of the Jewish birth and nursing of psychoanalysis in the *peculiar make-up of the Jew, who is analytical in a psychological sense, and who is constantly reflecting on the Why and Wherefore of everything,* as exemplified in the style of Ecclesiastes."[40] This impressionistic sense of what must be recognizably Jewish had long enjoyed a certain popularity within the psychoanalytic fraternity. In early 1907, at a meeting of the Vienna Psychoanalytic Society, Isidor Sadger, one of Freud's first followers, suggested that "the disposition of Jews to obsessive neuroses is perhaps connected with the addiction to brooding—*Grübelsucht*—characteristic of them for thousands of years." Sadger offered the study of the Talmud in evidence.[41] Later Ernest Jones, too, subscribed to the dubious notion that Jews have a peculiar "aptness for psychological intuition."[42]

Freud, though far from persuaded, was not unimpressed. But, as was his habit, he chose to generalize a parochial point to all of humanity. "We find obsessive neuroses among the

39. See Freud's brief discussion of Jewish "intellectuality" in *Moses and Monotheism, SE* XXIII, 111–15.

40. Roback, *Jewish Influences in Modern Thought,* 196–97.

41. Sadger at the Wednesday Psychological Society, January 30, 1907. *Protokolle,* I, 93.

42. Jones, *Free Associations,* 209.

normally most highly developed people," he commented on
Sadger's speculation about Jewish compulsiveness. The example
he offered was Emile Zola—not a Jew, of course—who, as a
fanatic for truth, had been an obsessional neurotic.[43] In the
very year he thus tersely deprived Jews of a monopoly on obsessive neuroses, Freud published his first paper on religion in
which he likened the obsessive ceremonials of neurotics to the
rituals of the devout. It was all of religion he was analyzing.
The enigma of his Jewish inheritance remained, for him, an
enigma, and remains for us too weak a reed to support the
complex and sprawling structure of psychoanalytic theory.

While the essence of his Jewish identity continued to resist Freud's analysis, he saw no obscurities in the contribution
sociology could make to its clarification. As a stranger to the
faith of his fathers and less than welcome in the culture that
surrounded him, he felt doubly alienated and saw himself as a
marginal man. This, Freud was convinced, had secured him
an inestimable advantage. His exclusion from "Austrianness"
at the university in the early 1870s, he later recalled, had
made him familiar in his youth with being in opposition and
thus prepared the way for "a certain independence of judgment."[44] He proposed as one crucial reason for the widespread,
obstructive, often venomous resistance to psychoanalysis that

43. Freud at the Wednesday Psychological Society, January 30, 1907.
Protokolle, I, 95.
44. "Selbstdarstellung," *GW* XIV, 35 / "Autobiographical Study," *SE*
XX, 9.

he, its founder, was a Jew—a Jew, moreover, who had never made a secret of his origins. But this supposed handicap had schooled him to accept, and profit from, solitude.[45] In his letter to B'nai B'rith, he expanded on this self-appraisal: he had discovered early "that I owe only to my Jewish nature the two characteristics that had become indispensable on my difficult life's way. Because I was a Jew, I found myself free from many prejudices which limited others in the employment of their intellects, and as a Jew I was prepared to go into opposition and to do without the agreement of the 'compact majority.'"[46] There were moments, then, when in his own way and for his own purposes, Freud borrowed the anti-Semites' charge that Jews are bound to be cleverer than the majority. But not always by any means: when he felt that his fellow-psychoanalysts had let him down, as he often did, he did not spare the Jews among them. It is a sign, small but telling, of his grip on a wider culture that in celebrating his ability to withstand the "compact majority," he drew on a gentile source: Henrik Ibsen's courageous, civic-minded physician in his *Enemy of the People*. Plainly, one did not have to be Jewish to be an enemy of the people. But Freud thought that at least it had helped him.

Freud's thesis is interesting and plausible, and it is buttressed by the obtrusive, much-noted fact that all the first

45. "Die Widerstände gegen die Psychoanalyse" (1925), *GW* XIV, 110 / "The Resistances to Psycho-Analysis," *SE* XIX, 222.

46. Freud to members of B'nai B'rith (May 6, 1926). *Briefe*, 381–82. That phrase, "compact majority," evidently resonated in his mind; he had already used it in his self-portrait, written two years earlier, also to recall his readiness to stand up against anti-Semites (see *GW* XIV, 35 / *SE* XX, 9).

psychoanalysts in Vienna were Jews. Ernest Jones, for one, accepted this sociological hypothesis without reserve. "I imagine," he wrote, reflecting on the Jewish phenomenon in psychoanalysis, "the reasons for this were mainly local ones in Austria and Germany, since, except to some slight extent in the United States, it is a feature that has not been repeated in any other country; in England, for example, only two analysts have been Jews (apart from refugee immigrants). In Vienna it was obviously easier for Jewish doctors to share Freud's ostracism, which was only an exacerbation of the life they were accustomed to, and the same was true of Berlin and Budapest, where anti-Semitism was almost equally pronounced."[47]

No doubt, one quality conspicuous in Freud's affirmation of his Jewishness is a brooding air of defiance. He was most Jewish when times were hardest for Jews. In 1873, when there was a surge of popular anti-Semitism in the wake of an economic collapse in Austria, and when, upon entering the university, he was "expected to feel inferior" as a Jew, he refused to comply: "I have never understood," he wrote, "why I should be ashamed of my descent or, as one began to say: my race."[48] Again, in 1897, when the persuasive, popular anti-Semitic demagogue Karl Lueger became mayor of Vienna, at the very time that Freud was developing his subversive theories, feeling desperately alone, Freud joined a newly formed B'nai B'rith lodge to be with his fellows. "That you are Jews could only be welcome to me," he told the brethren in 1926, recalling those early

47. Jones, *Free Associations*, 208–09.
48. "Selbstdarstellung," *GW* XIV, 34 / "Autobiographical Study," *SE* XX, 9.

days. "I was a Jew myself, and it has always seemed to me not only undignified, but quite nonsensical, to deny it."[49] In the same year, thinking of the contemporary political situation, he told an interviewer: "My language is German. My culture, my attainments, are German. I considered myself German intellectually, until I noticed the growth of anti-Semitic prejudice in German and German Austria. Since that time, I prefer to call myself a Jew."[50]

There can be little question that, in face of professional skepticism compounded by bigotry, a measure of toughness was a highly adaptive quality for the early psychoanalysts, not excluding Freud. It remained adaptive in Freud's later years. When he told his interviewer that, though by language and culture a German, he now preferred to call himself a Jew, he rather misrepresented the history of his identifications. He had in fact always called himself a Jew; what had been happening in the 1920s, with the emergence of Hitler in Germany and only marginally less revolting right-wing politicians in Austria, was that he had chosen to deny, in fact discard, the German facets of his selfhood. For the tactics and strategies of the psychoanalytic *movement,* then, Freud's being a Jew in an anti-Semitic culture is of real interest. The *origins* of psychoanalysis, though, are untouched by his historical situation. After all, Josef Breuer, whose patient Anna O. started it all, did not have the courage of his own discoveries and shied away from the sexual roots of her spectacular hysteria. And Breuer was a Jew.

49. Freud to the members of B'nai B'rith (May 6, 1926). *Briefe,* 381.
50. This interview was published four years later in book form in George Sylvester Viereck, *Glimpses of the Great* (1930), 34.

On the other side, Charles Darwin, whose work was as subversive as Freud's, was born, brought up, and lived securely within the English establishment.

A brief confrontation of Freud with Darwin may offer an escape from this maze. Charles Darwin was Freud's only real competitor as a modern cultural conquistador. His theories proved, like Freud's, profoundly offensive to reigning pieties and hence anxiety-producing in the extreme. If natural selection was true, it must have in the long run the most drastic consequences for the way men looked at the world, read sacred texts, conducted their business, thought about politics, even ordered their moral and marital lives. Like Freud, too, Darwin fully appreciated the scandal of his ideas and, despite occasional bouts of nerve at his daring, rather enjoyed it. Again like Freud, Darwin on occasion resorted to theological language: biologists responding to the *Origin of Species* were "converts," opponents were beset by "accursed religious bigotry."[51] Thus, very much in Freud's Enlightened camp, Darwin split the world into scientists and theologians.

Darwin and Freud had a good deal in common as well in their manner of enlisting support and encouraging their loyal

51. See Darwin to Joseph D. Hooker, June 17, 1856, January 3, 1860; Darwin to Charles Lyell, December 5, 1859; Darwin to A. R. Wallace, July 9, 1871, Francis Darwin, ed., *The Life and Letters of Charles Darwin*, 2 vols. (1887), I, 431–32; II, 54, 35, 323–24. Darwin to Hooker, September 16, 1871. Francis Darwin, ed., *More Letters of Charles Darwin*, 2 vols. (1903), I, 332–33.

troops. Darwin, as Freud would do later, thanked friends, acquaintances, and strangers for appreciative reviews and alerted his followers to valuable recruits or unforeseen antagonists. Yet Freud and Darwin differed, and differed decisively, in their fundamental attitude toward the controversies their theories generated. True, Darwin could get irritated with the unfavorable attention that devout scientists lavished on him; in his private correspondence he denounced them as "unfair" or, on occasion, as "spiteful" or even "illiberal" and "abusive."[52] The pious made him angry with their misrepresentations and their selective way of quoting from his writings. In 1860, a year after he had published the *Origin of Species,* he confided to his most combative lieutenant, T. H. Huxley, "I have got fairly sick of hostile reviews."[53] Darwin was no saint, and his critics' most critical reader. But he was largely spared the keen sense of isolation—somewhat overdone perhaps but not without substantial cause—that embittered Freud's early days of discovery and kept him from enjoying his international reputation in later years.

Freud did not refuse to learn from his detractors, nor did opposition shake his confidence in his theories. But he was less resilient, and far more exasperated with the world, than Darwin was. "Nothing which persons say hurts me for long,"

52. See Darwin to Charles Lyell, March 24, 1860. *Life and Letters,* II, 91; Darwin to J. S. Henslow, May 8, 1860. *More Letters,* I, 149; Darwin to Asa Gray, May 22, 1860. *Life and Letters,* II, 107; Darwin to J. D. Hooker. June 5, 1860, ibid., II, 110.

53. Darwin to T. H. Huxley, December 2, 1860. *Life and Letters,* II, 147.

Darwin wrote, knowing better than anyone how long and how intensely he had studied his evidence.[54] "I have been atrociously abused by my religious countrymen; but as I live an independent life in the country it does not in the least hurt me in any way."[55] Freud, perpetually worried about providing for his six children, did not live as a country gentleman, did not enjoy an independence. Admittedly, Darwin was protesting too much. His perpetual, wearing ill health, his crippling and unrelieved stomach and bowel symptoms, which the most diligent medical researchers have been unable to track to a physical cause, hint at the price he paid for his patience, his reasonableness, his generosity, his willingness to revise his formulations on the basis of well-informed and cogent criticism. Darwin's imperious need to work and his premature brooding on old age bear a close resemblance to Freud's long-lived symptomatic preoccupations. *"Nothing,"* Darwin declared, "is so intolerable as idleness."[56] Writing to a friend in 1839, he lamented, "Excuse this letter—I am very old and stupid"; again, two years later, "I am grown a dull old spiritless dog to what I used to be."[57] He was just entering his thirties. Still, after reading a long and penetrating essay on the *Origin* by the Scottish engineer Fleeming Jenkin, Darwin could conclude: "Fleeming Jenkin has given me much trouble, but has been of

54. Darwin to J. S. Henslow, May 14, 1860. *More Letters,* I, 150.

55. Darwin to J. L. A. Quatrefauges, July 11, 1862. Ibid., I, 202.

56. Sir Gavin de Beer, ed., *Darwin's Journal, Bulletin of the British Museum (Natural History),* Historical Series, II (1959), 9.

57. See Ralph Colp, *To Be an Invalid: The Illness of Charles Darwin* (1977), 23. Colp's study is the authoritative work on Darwin's health.

more real use to me than any other essay or review."[58] This is not a genial sentiment that would have come easily to Freud.

It is only too tempting to exaggerate Freud's rigidity. He was far more forbearing, far more receptive to dissent than most of his biographers, including benevolent biographers, have allowed. He could sustain across the decades friendships with the Protestant Pfister and with the existentialist psychiatrist Ludwig Binswanger. He could feel, and voice, open-minded, exuberant enthusiasm for the clinical and theoretical psychoanalytic innovations with which Otto Rank and Sándor Ferenczi worried more conventional analysts in the early 1920s. Freud, indeed, when the time came to part with Rank, was more reluctant to read him out of the analytic family than his exigent and humorless followers were. He remained on largely cordial terms with Ernest Jones right through the 1920s, even though Jones refused to adopt Freud's new theories on female sexuality and even appeared to Freud, the outraged father, to be engaged in a conspiracy with Melanie Klein to denigrate his daughter Anna's practice of child analysis.[59] The notorious quarrels in which Freud engaged during his career as an analyst, above all his parting with Adler and Jung, have been treated as so many excommunications, even though the available documents show that the provocations for these breaks did not principally come from Freud. "I'm not suitable as a cult object," he told Jung in 1907, and meant it.[60]

58. Darwin to J. D. Hooker, January 16, 1869. *More Letters*, II, 379.
59. See Freud to Ernest Jones, September 23, 1927. Freud Collection, D2, LC.
60. Freud to Jung, November 15, 1907. *Freud-Jung*, 108 (98).

But there is a militancy about Freud's quest for general acceptance that was far less marked in Darwin. While Darwin was satisfied with revising his work after further reflection and absorbing palpable hits by rational critics, while he trusted the passage of time and the weight of his argumentation, Freud orchestrated his wooing of the public mind through a loyal cadre of adherents, founded periodicals and wrote popularizations that would spread the authorized word, dominated international congresses of analysts until he felt too frail to attend them and after that through surrogates like his daughter Anna. "I do so hate controversy," Darwin wrote in 1871, when he had had more than a decade of it.[61] Freud was more ambivalent: there were times when he grew weary of contention, times when he professed to hate it. But it is hard to ward off the suspicion that once he had the enemy in his gunsight, he thrived on intellectual warfare.

To be sure, the needs of Darwin and Freud as organizers of opinion were not the same. Darwin had originated a radical theory in biology that public debate might refine and modify. Freud's material was more elusive, harder to duplicate or rediscover. What is more, Freud was practicing and propagating a therapy that could only benefit from conclaves of like-minded practitioners. Besides, while the implications of Darwin's views were threatening and unsettling, they were not quite so directly abrasive, not quite so unrespectable, as Freud's views on infantile sexuality, the ubiquity of perversions, and the dynamic power of unconscious urges. Whatever the historians' verdict

61. Darwin to A. R. Wallace, July 12, 1871. *Life and Letters,* II, 326.

on his plight as a revolutionary, Freud behaved more like a general marshaling his forces and mapping his movements than a scientist willing to let his ideas carry their own conviction. This is what kept the influential Swiss psychiatrist Eugen Bleuler, one of Freud's most desirable and most elusive catches, from remaining a member of the International Psychoanalytic Association. "In my opinion," he told Freud in 1911, "this 'who is not for us is against us,' this 'all or nothing,' is necessary for religious communities and useful for political parties. I can therefore understand the principle as such, but for science I consider it harmful."[62] Freud could not afford to take so objective, so disinterested, an attitude. He felt surrounded by a hostile, uncomprehending medical and psychiatric establishment, viciously slandered by Jew-haters, exasperated and exhausted by devious and troublesome deserters. Confronting malevolent priests, unreceptive physicians, intrusive journalists, timid ex-psychoanalysts, and implacable anti-Semites, Freud felt compelled, much like the philosophes two centuries before him, to stand ready for battle.

Whatever authority Freud's sociological argument for the Jewishness of psychoanalysis may claim rests on this bellicose stance and on his justifications for it. Some of these were realistic enough. Freud lived, in company with his Jewish followers, in a bewildering atmosphere. It was less fostering than grudging but not without its smiling prospects. Austrian society at the end of the nineteenth century was just anti-Semitic enough to deny Jews full social equality and frank, unbigoted

62. Bleuler to Freud, December 4, 1911. Freud Collection, D2, LC.

acceptance, but not anti-Semitic enough to keep them out of the universities and research institutes. It gave Jews an opportunity to study, invent, imagine with the rest of the educated population, but it forced them to intensify their search for cohesion, their rage to excel, their sheer need for success. Darwin, at home in his society, could unlike Freud afford to sit and wait.

The sociological argument, then, has a certain show of reason on its side. But Freud's thesis is far from complete and, when all is said, less than compelling. It invites the intriguing conjecture that in a society less virulently anti-Semitic than Freud's own—say, Britain or France, where most psychoanalysts were not Jewish—a gentile might have become the founder of Freud's science. Other, equally speculative considerations raise other, no less intriguing conjectures. To accept and profess his theory, Freud wrote in 1925, "called for a certain measure of readiness to accept a situation of solitary opposition—a situation with which nobody is more familiar than a Jew."[63] But marginality is a mixed blessing. In fact living on the margin leads as easily to conformism as to unconventionality; it may inhibit the spirit of invention rather than nourish it. After all, other Jews, just as marginal as Freud, had themselves baptized or went into business with their nominal Judaism intact; still others joined the Communist party, emigrated to the United States, or became Zionists. By and large they showed themselves no more intelligent or original than anyone else. I have shown that a believer, whether Jew or Christian, could never have founded

63. "Widerstände gegen die Psychoanalyse," *GW* XIV, 110 / "Resistances to Psycho-Analysis," *SE* XIX, 222.

psychoanalysis. That founder had to be too iconoclastic to accommodate religious faith. He had to be deeply immersed in religion as a phenomenon to be studied rather than a promise to pray for or a supreme reality to worship. It is no coincidence that Darwin, too, should have been an atheist. Hence it does not follow that only a marginal man, and in particular a marginal Jew, could have done Freud's life's work.

My survey has produced mainly negative results. The claims for the Jewishness of psychoanalysis based on its materials or its intellectual inheritance have proved to be without foundation. The claim for an elusive Jewish quality that somehow, mysteriously, informed Freud's work, a claim he seems to have endorsed, is too insubstantial to carry the weight some of his biographers have put upon it. "And we hail from there" all the same, Freud wrote in 1932 to his friend the novelist Arnold Zweig, about Palestine. "It is impossible to say what we have taken along in blood and nerves (as one incorrectly puts it) as a heritage from life in that country. Oh," he added, yearning for light on the subject, "life could be very interesting if one only knew and understood more about it."[64] It is a touching exclamation, understandable in light of his intensified anti-German animus. But it remains an impassioned, wishful guess, nothing more. Only the notion that the Jews' ambiguous social location in Freud's time and culture may have prodded them to distinguish themselves and stand out boldly against

64. Freud to Arnold Zweig, May 8, 1932. *The Letters of Sigmund Freud and Arnold Zweig* (1968; tr. Robson-Scott, 1970), 51–52 (40).

the "compact majority" has any shadow of merit. And the merit of that argument, too, is limited, compromised as it is by the plethora of counterexamples.

Freud, I conclude, was a Jew but not a Jewish scientist. I have no intention of imitating him by trying to take Freud away from his people as he tried to take away Moses. But the decisive distinction between personal identity and scientific allegiance remains intact. Writing to Ernest Jones in 1926 on the touchy subject of telepathy, in which he had taken a benevolent if somewhat quizzical interest for some years, Freud reported that he was more convinced than ever that there was something in it. Experiments he had performed with Ferenczi and with his daughter Anna "have gained such persuasive power for me, that diplomatic considerations had to take a back seat. Once again I saw a situation before me where I had to repeat, on a much reduced scale, the great experiment of my life, namely to stand up for a conviction without regarding the resonance of my surroundings. So, then, it was inevitable. If someone should reproach you with my Fall into Sin, you are free to reply that my adherence to telepathy is my private affair, like my Jewishness, my passion for smoking and other things, and the theme of telepathy—inessential for psychoanalysis."[65] Inessential: *wesensfremd*—his Judaism was inessential, not to Freud, but to his creation, psychoanalysis.

This attitude emerges forcefully, if rather poignantly, in Freud's last sustained and perhaps most controversial work,

65. Freud to Jones, March 7, 1926. Freud Collection, D2, LC.

Moses and Monotheism, the three linked essays he published not long before his death. The *Moses* aroused a storm of protest in Jewish circles everywhere. He was deluged by reviews and by a very avalanche of letters, most of them from strangers, calling him to account for the enormity he had committed. Anxious scholars visited him in London to talk him out of publishing the book; others wrote no less anxious letters to the same purpose. In a time of terrible travail, with the Nazi persecution of the Jews in Germany and Austria intensifying beyond the bounds of the most vicious czarist pogroms, Freud had dared to call Moses an Egyptian and to claim that the Jews had murdered him. Scholars like Martin Buber were openly disdainful: Freud, Buber held, had based his conjectures on feeble, uncertain evidence and failed to consult relevant authorities. He had written what Freud himself had called a "novel," and the result was, his correspondents bluntly informed him, a disaster, an act of betrayal. One anonymous critic from Boston unburdened himself in a sequence of breathless, furious paragraphs: "I read in the local press your statement that Moses was not a Jew. / It is to be regretted that you could not go to your grave without disgracing youself, you old nitwit. / We have renegades like you by the thousands, we are glad we are rid of them and hope soon to be rid of you. / It is to be regretted that the Gangsters in Germany did not put you into a concentration camp, that's where you belong."[66] Most of Freud's other mail was more civilized but just marginally less severe. Only his most consistent and uncritical admirers, like

66. Anonymous to Freud, May 26, 1939. Freud Museum, London.

Arnold Zweig or Max Eitingon, found Freud's arguments persuasive and his defiant gesture of publishing the book quite in order.

Not surprisingly, Freud's prolonged and intense preoccupation with Moses in the mid-1930s has called forth diverse, sometimes contradictory, psychoanalytic readings of his mind. Freud made Moses an Egyptian so that he, Freud, could be the first true Moses to his people. Freud made Moses an Egyptian and stressed his principal role in the Exodus, that flight from persecution, to dramatize his own independence from both his Jewish heritage and his German culture. Freud made Moses the sole shaper of the Jewish character, the giver of monotheism to his people, that he might identify himself with such a mighty lawgiver. Freud, the world's first and most embattled psychoanalyst, was willing to maintain that Moses had been murdered by his superstitious and rebellious Jewish followers to reenact his own fate at the hand of his renegade disciples and destructive critics.

Not all of these probes into the recesses of Freud's psyche are necessarily wide of the mark. Since glimpsing the *Moses* of Michelangelo on his first visit to Rome in 1901, he had been fascinated with this superhuman figure and identified with his great mission, volcanic temper, and splendid efforts at self-control. But neither the roots of *Moses and Monotheism* in Freud's repressed past, nor for that matter its merits—or defects—is at issue in these chapters. What matters here is the dazzling light that Freud's brooding on Moses throws on his way with scientific problems and on his priorities.

Freud was an investigator haunted by ideas. When an

enigma took hold of him, he was plunged into torment. Struck by the surprising resemblance between the first scene of *King Lear,* Portia's choice among three caskets in *The Merchant of Venice,* and the judgment of Paris, he worried it through until the answer stood before him, lucid and obvious after the fact. Growing dissatisfied in the early 1920s with psychoanalytic ideas on female sexuality, he inquired and reasoned and argued until he had developed propositions that, to his mind, at least addressed the mystery that is woman. His famous query to Marie Bonaparte, "What does woman want?," was not playful or frivolous; it was virtually a cry of despair, the desolate exclamation of a decoder staring at a document he cannot decipher. The only thing that gave him peace when he was in the grip of a riddle was to find its solution.[67] The question of just what, or who, had made the Jews Jewish was such a riddle for Freud. In the poisonous atmosphere of modern anti-Semitism in Central Europe, it was a natural question to arise. Under its pressure all other considerations must be set aside. Moses, as he put it himself, "tormented me like an unlaid ghost."[68]

A formula suggests itself: when Freud's loyalties to Judaism and to science clashed, Judaism would have to give way. But, like most formulas, this one would gravely oversimplify the matter. Freud was not disposed to let others define his Jewishness for him. It remains true, though, that he was ready to offend Jews when science called. He could not, after all, escape

67. I am planning to discuss and fully document this characteristic of Freud's in a biography, *Freud: A Life for Our Time* (forthcoming).

68. *Der Mann Moses und die monotheistische Religion* (1939), *GW* XVI, 210 / *Moses and Monotheism, SE* XXIII, 103.

or deny the anger, irritation, and dismay he was arousing among his fellow-Jews. "Just half an hour ago," he reported to Arnold Zweig in June 1938, "the mail brought me a letter from a young Jewish American, in which I am begged not to rob our poor, unhappy people—*Volksgenossen*—of the one consolation that has remained to them in their misery. The letter was pleasant and well-meaning, but what an overestimation!" His treatise, he thought, was too dry to disturb the beliefs of a single believer, even if the book should happen to reach him.[69] *Moses and Monotheism,* he warned half a year later, when a Hebrew translation seemed in the offing, "is a continuation of the theme of *Totem and Taboo* in application to Jewish religious history. But I ask you to consider that its contents are particularly suitable to wound Jewish feelings, in so far as they do not want to subordinate themselves to science."[70] He professed distress at the response of his fellow-Jews: "Naturally," he wrote, he did not enjoy offending them. "But what can I do about it? I have filled my whole life with standing up for what I considered to be the scientific truth, even when it was uncomfortable and disagreeable to my fellowmen. I cannot close it with an act of disavowal."[71]

This conviction governed his life, always. On a Friday afternoon in the summer of 1938, in London, not long after Freud had been rescued from Nazified Vienna, a young Oxford phi-

69. Freud to Arnold Zweig, June 28, 1838. *Freud-Zweig,* 172 (163). In his mordant irony, Freud uses the old term *Volksgenossen,* literally "comrades belonging to the same people," for his fellow-Jews, purloined by the Nazis.
70. Freud to J. Dwossis, December 11, 1938. Freud Museum, London.
71. Freud to Charles Singer, October 31, 1938. *Briefe,* 469.

losopher came to call. They talked of psychoanalysis in Britain, of Freud's recent adventures in Austria after the Anschluss. As it came to be around five in the afternoon, Martha Freud joined them and said to the visitor, "You must know that on Friday evenings good Jewish women light candles for the approach of the Sabbath. But this monster—*Unmensch*—will not allow this, because he says that religion is a superstition." Freud gravely nodded and agreed: "Yes," he said, "it *is* a superstition," to which the Frau Professor, addressing her visitor, rejoined: "You see?" In retrospect, their guest, perceptive but generous, thought the indignation humorous, mingled with obvious affection, a standing joke, repeated for half a century for the benefit of sympathetic visitors.[72]

But we know—Freud has taught us—that jokes are rarely just funny. After his death, his widow would tell friends that through all her married life, a long time together, not a harsh word had fallen between them.[73] Yet Martha Freud had retained a trace of indignation, perhaps of sadness, in the presence of the imperious atheist who had so many years ago swept her away from her family and, more painfully, from her faithfully practiced religious observances. For Freud himself the joke had its serious ingredient. Yes, religion *was* a superstition, and one does not make a science with a superstition. He had said it all in 1927, concluding his *Future of an Illusion,* in the stirring

72. Private communication to the author, May 8, 1984.
73. See Martha Freud to Ludwig Binswanger, November 7, 1939, and Martha Freud to Paul Federn, n.d. (early November, 1939). Both by permission of Sigmund Freud Copyrights, Wivenhoe.

passage I have quoted before: "No, our science is no illusion. But an illusion it would be to believe that we could get anywhere else what it cannot give us."

❁ BIBLIOGRAPHY
AND INDEX

BIBLIOGRAPHY

I have divided this bibliography into three parts: the collections of manuscripts I consulted, the titles I cite or quote in the text (offering some comments on a number of them), and other books and articles that proved instructive, stimulating, worth criticizing, in one way or another valuable in the writing of this book. This third section makes no claim to completeness; especially as I sketched out the "warfare between science and religion" for the introduction and dealt with Freud's Jewish environment in chapter 3, I worked with more material than I have had room to mention here. While I have listed the authors alphabetically in the usual way, I have organized them chronologically if there are several entries under one author.

I. Manuscript Collections

Archives of the British Psycho-Analytical Society, London
Correspondence between Anna Freud and Ernest Jones (Jones Papers).

Sigmund Freud Copyrights, Wivenhoe.
Correspondence between Freud and Ludwig Binswanger, Max Eitingon, Ernest Jones, Oskar Pfister, and Stefan Zweig, and some miscellaneous letters.

Freud Museum, London
Miscellaneous letters from and to Freud, from and to correspondents in Palestine and elsewhere.

Manuscript Division, Library of Congress, Washington, D.C.
Correspondence between Freud and Eugen Bleuler and Sándor Ferenczi, letters to Eduard Silberstein and other miscellaneous correspondents.

II. Titles Cited and Quoted in the Text

Abderhalden, Emil. "Sigmund Freuds Einstellung zur Religion." *Ethik*, V (1928–29), 91–101.

Amsel, Avrohom. *Judaism and Psychology* (1969).

————. *Rational Irrational: Man Torah Psychology* (1976). Pious Jewish psychology explicitly contrasted with Freud's impieties.

Anderson, Camilla M. *Beyond Freud: A Creative Approach to Mental Health* (1958). An essay by a Christian physician.

Bakan, David. *Sigmund Freud and the Jewish Mystical Tradition* (1958). See my critical comments in the text, pp. 130–31.

Bakhtin, Mikhail. *Le Freudisme* (1927; tr. into French by Guy Verret, 1980). An important Marxist critique of psychoanalysis, most probably wholly or largely by Bakhtin, though the name of his associate Volochinov is on the title page. (For the controversy over authorship, see Katerina Clark and Michael Holquist below.)

Balmary, Marie. *Psychoanalyzing Psychoanalysis: Freud and the Hidden Fault of the Father* (1979; tr. Ned Lukacher, 1982). A highly critical, imaginative effort to turn Freud's methods on Freud and to portray him as wrestling with oedipal issues all his life; it concentrates on what Balmary reads as his contradictions, omissions, and inconsistencies.

Barta, Johannes. *Jüdische Familienerziehung: Das jüdische Erziehungswesen im 19. und 20. Jahrhundert* (1974). Surveys the question of "family education" among modern Jewry in its cultural and political context, but includes schools as well.

Baruk, Henri. "La signification de la psychanalyse et le Judaïsme." *Revue d'Histoire de la Médecine Hébraïque*, XIX (1965), 15–28, 53–65.

Biddle, W. Earl. *Integration of Religion and Psychiatry* (1956). A brave attempt by a believing physician.

Birk, Kasimir. *Sigmund Freud und die Religion* (1970). A careful survey of the Roman Catholic response to Freud's views on faith.

Brierley, Marjorie. *Trends in Psycho-Analysis* (1951).

Buber, Martin. *Briefwechsel aus sieben Jahrzehnten*. Edited by Grete Schaeder, 3 vols. (1972–75). A fine, if not wholly complete edition with an excellent long introductory essay by the editor.

Cassirer, Ernst. *The Philosophy of the Enlightenment* (1932; tr. Fritz C. A. Koelln and James P. Pettegrove, 1951). A classic.

Chadwick, Owen. *The Secularization of the European Mind in the Nineteenth Century* (1975). A highly personal, immensely stimulating romp through European religious history by an eminent English church historian.

Charteris, Evan. *The Life and Letters of Sir Edmund Gosse* (1931). Now largely superseded by Ann Thwaite's biography (see below).

Clark, Katerina, and Michael Holquist. *Mikhail Bakhtin* (1984).

Clark, Ronald. *Freud: The Man and the Cause* (1980). A large-scale biography, strongest on Freud's personal life.

Colp, Ralph. *To Be an Invalid: The Illness of Charles Darwin* (1977). The standard work on Darwin's many ailments.

Condillac, Étienne Bonnot de. *Traité des systèmes* (1751). In *Oeuvres*, edited by Georges Le Roy, 3 vols. (1947–51), vol. I.

Cornell, John. "What is a religious painting?" (manuscript, 1986). An able study of German religiosity at the turn of the century.

Darwin, Francis, ed. *The Life and Letters of Charles Darwin*. 2 vols. (1887).

———. *More Letters of Charles Darwin*. 2 vols. (1903).

de Beer, Sir Gavin, ed. *Darwin's Journal, Bulletin of the British Museum (Natural History)*. Historical Series, II (1959).

Diderot, Denis. "Encyclopédie." In *Oeuvres complètes*, edited by Jules

Assézat and Maurice Tourneux, 20 vols. (1875–77), XIV, 414–503.

———. "Fait." In ibid., XV, 1–6.

———. *Correspondance.* Edited by Georges Roth, 16 vols. (1955–70).

Draper, John William. *History of the Conflict between Religion and Science* (1874).

Du Bois-Reymond, Emil. "Voltaire als Naturforscher" (1868). In *Reden von Emil du Bois-Reymond,* 2 vols., edited by Estelle Du Bois-Reymond (1885; 2d enlarged ed., 1912), I, 318–48.

———. "Über die Grenzen des Naturerkennens" (1872), ibid., I, 441–73.

———. "Darwin und Kopernicus" (1883), ibid., II, 243–48.

———. "Zu Diderots Gedächtnis" (1884), ibid., II, 285–300.

Engels, Friedrich. *Socialism: Utopian and Scientific* (tr. Edward Aveling, 1892, ed. 1935).

Feuerbach, Ludwig. *Das Wesen des Christenthums* (1841; 2d ed., 1843). (Translated as *The Essence of Christianity* by George Eliot, 1854.)

Fleming, Donald. *John William Draper and the Religion of Science* (1950). The standard life.

Franzblau, Abraham N. In *Judaism and Psychiatry: Two Approaches to the Personal Problems and Needs of Modern Man,* edited by Simon Noveck (1956). A pastoral psychiatrist in search of accommodation between the two fields of the title.

Freud, Anna. "Inaugural Lecture" (August 1977). *Int. Jl. of Psycho-Anal.,* LIX (1978), 145–48.

———. Introductory note in *Freud-Pfister* (see below).

Freud, Harry, interview with Richard Dyck. "Mein Onkel Sigmund." *Aufbau,* May 11, 1956, p. 3. Revealing but not wholly reliable.

Freud, Martin. "Who was Freud?" In *The Jews of Austria: Essays on their Life, History and Destruction,* ed. Josef Fraenkel (1967), 197–211.

Freud, Sigmund. *Traumdeutung* (1900), *Gesammelte Werke* (henceforth, *GW*), II–III / *The Interpretation of Dreams, Standard Edition* (henceforth *SE*), IV, V.

————. "Obituary of Professor S. Hammerschlag" (1904), *SE* IX, 255–56. A touching tribute to Freud's religion teacher.

————. *Der Witz und seine Beziehung zum Unbewussten* (1905), *GW* VI / *Jokes and their Relation to the Unconscious, SE* VI.

————. *Drei Abhandlungen zur Sexualtheorie* (1905; 6th ed. 1925), *GW* V, 29–145 / *Three Essays on the Theory of Sexuality, SE* VII, 123–243.

————. "Contribution to a Questionnaire on Reading" (1907), *SE* IX, 245–47.

————. "Bemerkungen über einen Fall von Zwangsneurose" (1909), *GW,* VII 381–463 / "Notes upon a Case of Obsessional Neurosis," *SE* X, 153–318.

————. "Bemerkungen über die Übertragungsliebe" (1915), *GW* X, 306–21 / "Observations on Transference Love," *SE* XII, 157–71.

————. "Eine Schwierigkeit der Psychoanalyse" (1917), *GW* XII, 3–12 / "A Difficulty in the Path of Psycho-Analysis," *SE* XVII, 135–44.

————. "Aus der Geschichte einer infantilen Neurose" (written 1914, published 1918), *GW* XII, 29–157 / "From the History of an Infantile Neurosis," *SE* XVII, 3–122.

————. "Selbstdarstellung" (written 1924, published 1925), *GW* XIV, 33–96 / "An Autobiographical Study," *SE* XX, 3–70.

————. "Die Widerstände gegen die Psychoanalyse" (1925), *GW* XIV, 99–110 / "The Resistances to Psycho-Analysis," *SE* XIX, 211–22.

————. *Die Frage der Laienanalyse* (1926), *GW* XIV, 209–96 / *The Question of Lay Analysis, SE* XX, 179–250.

————. *Die Zukunft einer Illusion* (1927), *GW* XIV, 325–80 / *The Future of an Illusion, SE* XXI, 1–56.

————. "A Religious Experience" (1928), *SE* XXI, 167–72 (in English in the original).

————. *Das Unbehagen in der Kultur* (1930), *GW* XIV, 419–506 / *Civilization and Its Discontents, SE* XXI, 59–145.

————. "Über eine Weltanschauung," *Neue Folge der Vorlesungen zur Einführung in die Psychoanalyse* (1932), *GW* XV, 170–97 / "The Question of a Weltanschauung," *New Introductory Lectures on Psycho-Analysis, SE* XXII, 158–82.

————. "Preface to the Hebrew Translation" of *Totem and Taboo* (written 1930, published 1934), *SE* XIII, xv.

————. *Der Mann Moses und die monotheistische Religion: Drei Abhand-lungen* (1939), *GW* XVI, 101–246 / *Moses and Monotheism: Three Essays, SE* XXIII, 1–137.

————. *Briefe 1873–1939,* ed. Ernst L. and Lucie Freud (1960; 2d ed., 1968). English version, *Letters of Sigmund Freud, 1873–1939,* tr. Tania and James Stern (1975).

Freud, Sigmund, and Karl Abraham. *Briefe 1907–1926.* Edited by Hilda C. Abraham and Ernst L. Freud (1965; tr. Bernard Marsh and Hilda C. Abraham under the title *A Psycho-Analytic Dialogue, The Letters of Sigmund Freud and Karl Abraham, 1907–1926* [1965]). Severely cut, these letters must be read in conjunction with the unpublished letters in the Abraham Papers, Library of Congress, Washington.

Freud, Sigmund, and Wilhelm Fliess. *Sigmund Freud. Briefe an Wilhelm Fliess, 1887–1904. Ungekürzte Ausgabe.* Edited by Jeffrey Mousaieff Masson, with work on this edition by Michael Schröter and transcriptions by Gerhard Fichtner (1986). The English version appeared a year earlier (1985) under the title *The Complete Letters of Sigmund Freud to Wilhelm Fliess, 1887–1904,* same editor, but the German edition has superior notes.

Freud, Sigmund, and C. G. Jung. *Briefwechsel* (1974). The English version, tr. Ralph Manheim for the Freud letters and R. F. C.

Hull for Jung's, appeared under the title *The Freud/Jung Letters. The Correspondence between Sigmund Freud and C. G. Jung,* edited by William McGuire (1974). McGuire's editing is impeccable; Manheim's translations are markedly superior to Hull's, who is far too free.

Freud, Sigmund, and Oskar Pfister. *Briefe 1909–1939.* Edited by Ernst L. Freud and Heinrich Meng (1963). The English version appeared under the title *Psycho-Analysis and Faith: The Letters of Sigmund Freud and Oskar Pfister,* tr. Eric Mosbacher (1963). A woefully incomplete edition, to be eked out with the unpublished letters in Sigmund Freud Copyrights, Wivenhoe.

Freud, Sigmund, and Arnold Zweig. *Briefwechsel.* Edited by Ernst L. Freud (1968). English version: *The Letters of Sigmund Freud and Arnold Zweig,* tr. Professor W. R. and Mrs. Robson-Scott (1970). What I said about the Freud-Abraham and Freud-Pfister correspondence applies here. The unpublished letters between the two are in Sigmund Freud Copyrights, Wivenhoe.

Fromm, Erich. *Psychoanalysis and Religion* (1950). A well-written popular text.

Garbett, Cyril Forster, Bishop of Southwark. "Introduction." In *Psychology and the Church* (1925), edited by O. Hardman, ix–xiv.

Gay, Peter. *Voltaire's Politics: The Poet as Realist* (1959).

———. *The Enlightenment: An Interpretation,* 2 vols. (*The Rise of Modern Paganism* [1966], and *The Science of Freedom* [1969]).

Gomperz, Theodor. *Essays und Erinnerungen* (1905).

Griffiths, Richard. *The Reactionary Revolution: The Catholic Revival in French Literature, 1870–1914* (1966). An authoritative study of such writers as Joris-Karl Huysmans, Charles Péguy, Paul Claudel, and others.

Haeckel, Ernst. *The Riddle of the Universe* (1899; tr. Joseph McCabe, 1900). A once famous text in the antireligious school by the German biologist and "Monist" philosopher.

Hale, Nathan G., Jr., ed. *James Jackson Putnam and Psychoanalysis: Letters between Putnam and Sigmund Freud, Ernest Jones, William James, Sándor Ferenczi and Morton Prince, 1877–1917* (1971). A splendid, thoughtfully edited collection, also transcribing Freud's letters in the original.

Hausdorff, Don. *Erich Fromm* (1972). Has some good material, especially on Fromm's early life.

Hoffer, Willi. Obituary of Oskar Pfister. *Int. Jl. of Psycho-Anal.*, XXXIX (1958), 616–17.

Hume, David. *A History of England from the Invasion of Julius Caesar to the Revolution in 1688* (1754–62; 8 vol. ed. 1780).

Huxley, Leonard, ed. *Life and Letters of Thomas Henry Huxley*, 2 vols. (1900).

James, Henry, ed. *The Letters of William James*, 2 vols. (1920).

James, William. "Reflex Action and Theism" (1881). In *The Will to Believe and Other Essays in Popular Philosophy* (1897), 111–44.

————. "The Will to Believe" (1896), in ibid., 1–31.

————. *The Varieties of Religious Experience: A Study in Human Nature* (1902).

Jones, Ernest. *The Life and Work of Sigmund Freud*, 3 vols. (1953–57). Still, with all its flaws, the standard biography.

————. *Free Associations: Memories of a Psycho-Analyst* (1959). Very interesting if not wholly candid.

Kaplan, Mordecai M. *Judaism as a Civilization: Toward a Reconstruction of American-Jewish Life* (1934; ed. 1967).

Katz, Robert L. "Aspects of Pastoral Psychology and the Rabbinate." A pamphlet reprint from *Pastoral Psychology*, V (October 1954), 7 unnumbered pages. An authoritative if brief survey.

————. *Empathy: Its Nature and Uses* (1963). An interesting psychological and religious study.

————. "Becoming a Friend to Myself: With a Little Help from Sigmund Freud, Erich Fromm, and Martin Buber." In *Jews in a*

Free Society: Challenges and Opportunities (1978), edited by Edward A. Goldman, 84–102. An eclectic essay.

Kautsky, Karl. *Die materialistische Geschichtsauffassung*, 2 vols. (1927).

Klein, Joel. *Psychology Encounters Judaism* (1979). In this encounter, Freud (that is the psychology in question) loses hands down.

Küng, Hans. *Freud and the Problem of God* (tr. Edward Quinn, 1979). A conciliatory series of lectures, from a very different perspective from this book.

Kushner, Martin. *Freud—A Man Obsessed* (1967). The title suggests the animus of this diatribe.

Lee, R. S. *Freud and Christianity* (1948; ed. 1967). Perhaps the most convincing (or least unconvincing) attempt to bring Freud and Christ together.

Liebman, Fan Loth. "Preface" (dated 1965) to Joshua Loth Liebman, *Hope for Man: An Optimistic Philosophy and Guide to Self-Fulfillment* (1966). A widow's paean.

Liebman, Joshua Loth. *Peace of Mind* (1946). The rabbi's amazing "Freudian" best-seller in the mid-1940s and later.

———, ed. *Psychiatry and Religion* (1948). A companion piece.

———. *Hope for Man,* See Liebman, Fan Loth.

Marr, G. Simpson. *Sex in Religion: An Historical Survey* (1936).

Mava do Valle, Maria Alice, Orlando Silva Santos, Francisco Alvim, Pedro Luzes. "Four Recently Discovered Letters by Freud to a Portuguese Correspondent. A Contribution to the Pre-History of Psycho-Analysis in Portugal." *Int. Rev. of Psycho-Anal.,* VI (1979), 437–40.

McCloy, Shelby T. *Gibbon's Hostility to Christianity* (1933).

McDougall, William. *Is America Safe for Democracy?* (1921).

———. *Psycho-Analysis and Social Psychology* (1936). Opinionated, influential, not wholly hostile.

Marx, Karl. Introduction to "Contribution to the Critique of Hegel's *Philosophy of Right.*" In *The Marx-Engels Reader,* edited by Robert C. Tucker (1972; 2d ed., 1978), 53–65.

Meissner, W. W. *Psychoanalysis and Religious Experience* (1984). A thoughtful recent treatment, quite different from my own.

Niebuhr, Reinhold. *The Nature and Destiny of Man: A Christian Interpretation,* 2 vols. (1941, 1943).

Noveck, Simon, see Franzblau, Abraham N.

Nunberg, Herman, and Ernst Federn, eds. *Protokolle der Wiener Psychoanalytischen Vereinigung,* 4 vols. (1976–81). The English version of these "protocols" first appeared under the title *Minutes of the Vienna Psychoanalytic Society* (1962–75). Important source.

Outler, Albert C. *Psychotherapy and the Christian Message* (1954).

Pfennigsdorf, Emil. *Praktische Theologie,* 2 vols. (1929–30).

Pfister, Oskar. "Das Elend unserer wissenschaftlichen Glaubenslehre." *Schweizerische theologische Zeitschrift,* XXI (1905), fascicle 4.

———. "Die Psychoanalyse als wissenschaftliches Prinzip und als seelsorgerische Methode." *Evangelische Freiheit,* X (1910), 66–73, 102–13, 137–46, 190–200.

———. *Die Frömmigkeit des Grafen Ludwig von Zinzendorf* (1910; 2d ed. 1925).

———. *Love in Children and Its Aberrations. A Book for Parents and Teachers* (1922; tr. Eden and Cedar Paul, 1924).

———. "Oskar Pfister." In *Die Pädagogik der Gegenwart in Selbstdarstellungen,* edited by Erich Hahn, 2 vols. (1926–27), II, 161–207.

———. "Neutestamentliche Seelsorge und psychoanalytische Therapie." *Imago,* XX (1934), 425–43.

———. *Christianity and Fear: A Study in the History and in the Psychology and Hygiene of Religion* (1944; tr. W. H. Johnston, 1948).

Philp, H. C. *Freud and Religious Belief* (1956). Another representative of this large genre.

Piper, Otto A. *The Christian Interpretation of Sex* (1942).

Pius XII. "Die sittlichen Grenzen der ärztlichen Forschungs- und Behandlungsmethoden." Speech of September 14, 1952, excerpted in *Die Rezeption der Psychoanalyse in der Soziologie, Psychologie und Theologie im deutschsprachigen Raum bis 1940,* edited by Johannes Cremerius (1981), 296.

Roazen, Paul. *Erik H. Erikson: The Power and Limits of a Vision* (1976).

Roback, A. A. *Jewish Influences in Modern Thought* (1929). One of the most determined efforts to make Freud's into a Jewish science.

Robert, Marthe. *From Oedipus to Moses: Freud's Jewish Identity* (1974; tr. Ralph Manheim, 1976). Elegantly argued, well informed, a valuable counterpoise to such interpretations as Bakan's; but excessively inclined to read Freud's "Jewish identity" in terms of his intimate, familial experience.

Roberts, Henry L. *Russia and America: Dangers and Prospects* (1956).

Rosen, George. "Freud and Medicine in Vienna." In *Freud: The Man, His World, His Influence,* edited by Jonathan Miller (1972), 21–39. Brief, but much the most perceptive treatment of Freud's medical world.

Rosenberg, Stuart E. *More Loves than One: The Bible Confronts Psychiatry* (1963). Expresses mixed feelings about Freud.

Rosenzweig, Franz. *Briefe und Tagebücher.* Edited by Rachel Rosenzweig and Edith Rosenzweig-Scheinmann, with collaboration of Bernhard Casper, 2 vols. (1979). The best edition by far.

Scharfenberg, Joachim. *Sigmund Freud und seine Religionskritik als Herausforderung für den christlichen Glauben* (1968; 3d ed. 1971). An excellent, beautifully informed essay which, from a Christian perspective, tries to see Freud straight.

Schwaber, Paul. "Title of Honor: The Psychoanalytic Congress in Jerusalem." *Midstream,* XXIV (March 1978), 26–35. A vivid account of the International Congress of 1977, scene of the reading of Anna Freud's controversial statement concerning psychoanalysis as a Jewish science.

Silber, Abba Hillel. *Where Judaism Differed: An Inquiry into the Distinctiveness of Judaism* (1961). Has a couple of appreciative (and rather surprising) sentences about psychoanalysis.

Steinberg, Milton. *From the Sermons of Rabbi Milton Steinberg: High Holydays* (sic!) *and Major Festivals.* Edited by Bernard Mandelbaum (1954). Drafts, often quite sketchy ones, but quite revealing.

Stekel, Wilhelm. *The Autobiography of Wilhelm Stekel: The Life Story of a Pioneer Psychoanalyst.* Edited by Emil A. Gutheil (1950). To be used with care.

Storfer, A. J. "Einige Stimmen zu Sigm. Freuds 'Zukunft einer Illusion.'" *Imago,* XIV (1928), 377–82. Helpful, brief.

Tillich, Paul. "The Idea and the Ideal of Personality" (1929). In *The Protestant Era* (tr. James Luther Adams, 1951), 115–35.

——. "The Theological Significance of Existentialism and Psychoanalysis" (1955). In *Theology of Culture,* edited by Robert C. Kimball (1959), 112–25. A sweeping statement.

Tournier, Paul. *Guilt and Grace: A Psychological Study* (1958; tr. Arthur W. Heathcote and others, 1962).

——. *The Whole Person in a Broken World* (1947; tr. John and Helen Doberstein, 1965). The physician as believer, both somewhat admiring and very skeptical of Freud.

Turgot, Anne-Robert-Jacques, baron d'Aulne. *Oeuvres de Turgot et documents le concernant.* Edited by G. Schelle, 5 vols. (1913–23).

Viereck, George Sylvester. *Glimpses of the Great* (1930).

Volochinov, V. N., see Bakhtin, Mikhail.

Voltaire. *Lettres philosophiques sur les Anglais* (1734; many editions).

——. *Notebooks.* Edited by Theodore Besterman, 2 vols. continuously paginated (1952).

Wartofsky, Marx W. *Feuerbach* (1977). The best modern study.

Werman, David S. "Sigmund Freud and Romain Rolland." *Int. Rev. of Psycho-Anal.,* IV (1977), 225–41.

White, Andrew Dixon. *Autobiography,* 2 vols. (1900).

Wittels, Fritz. *Sigmund Freud: The Man, His Personality and His School* (1924; tr. Eden and Cedar Paul, 1924). The first biography, filled with errors but far from useless.

Zilboorg, Gregory. "Psyche, Soul and Religion." Last chapter of *Mind, Medicine and Man* (originally published in 1943), in Zilboorg, *Psychoanalysis and Religion*, edited by Margaret Stone Zilboorg (1967), 19–53.

———. "Scientific Psychopathology and Religious Issues" (1953). In ibid., 104–16.

———. "Love in Freudian Psychoanalysis" (1953). In ibid., 117–39.

III. Other Titles of Interest

Andrea, Stefan. *Pastoraltheologische Aspekte der Lehre Sigmund Freuds von der Sublimierung der Sexualität* (1974). A "refutation" of Freud from a Roman Catholic point of view.

Anzieu, Didier. *Freud's Self-Analysis* (1959; 2d ed., 1975; tr. Peter Graham, 1986). Exhaustive study of Freud's younger years, mainly through his dreams.

Barzun, Jacques. *A Stroll with William James* (1983). An appealing plea for James by a stylish admirer.

Bergmann, Martin S. "Moses and the Evolution of Freud's Jewish Identity." *The Israel Annals of Psychiatry and Related Disciplines*, XIV (March 1976), 3–26. An important article; judicious, sensitive, and comprehensive.

Bitter, Wilhelm, ed. *Vorträge über das Vaterproblem in Psychotherapie, Religion und Gesellschaft* (1954). Though mainly Jungian in orientation, it contains some material from a Freudian perspective.

Boyer, John W. *Political Radicalism in Late Imperial Vienna: Origins of the Christian Social Movement, 1848–1897* (1981). An excellent, detailed account of the political culture in which Viennese anti-Semitism flourished.

Buber, Martin. "Schuld und Schuldgefühle" (1957). In *Werke*, I (1962), 475–502. One of the rare published references in Buber to Freud.

Cockshut, A. O. J., ed. *Religious Controversies of the 19th Century: Selected Documents* (1966). A fine anthology containing contentious texts bearing up my discussion of the war between science and religion.

Cronbach, Abraham. "The Psychoanalytic Study of Judaism." *Hebrew Union College Annual*, VIII–IX (1931–32), 605–745. Detailed, uninspired survey.

Cuddihy, John Murray. *The Ordeal of Civility: Freud, Marx, Lévi-Strauss, and the Jewish Struggle with Modernity* (1974). Wrestles manfully in part I with Freud's secularism, but as he thinks of Freud as an *"Ostjude"* (p. 17), Cuddihy falls into predictable confusions. His identification of "id" with "yid"—the Jew is hated because he represents unacceptable impulses to others—is, questions of taste apart, quite debatable.

Darwin, Charles. *The Correspondence of Charles Darwin*, I, *1821–1836*, edited by Frederick Burkhardt and Sydney Smith (1985). A great edition in progress; will supersede all earlier collections.

Dittes, James E. "Beyond William James." In *Beyond the Classics? Essays in the Scientific Study of Religion* (1973), edited by Charles Y. Glock and Phillip E. Hammond, 291–349. An outstanding paper on James's religious thought by a prominent psychologist of religion.

Dolles, Wilhelm. *Das Jüdische und das Christliche als Geistesrichtung* (n.d., 1925?). An attack on psychoanalysis as principally Jewish.

Feinstein, Howard M. *Becoming William James* (1984). A psychological, at times psychoanalytic account of James's growth as man and thinker.

Flugel, J. C. *Man, Morals and Society: A Psycho-Analytic Study* (1945). Argues that Freud's thought has done much to undermine, but not to disprove, religion.

———. Review of Marjorie Brierley, *Trends in Psycho-Analysis, Int. Jl. of Psycho-Anal.*, XXXII (1951), 259–61. Generally favorable but not wholly uncritical.

Forsyth, David. *Psychology and Religion: A Study by a Medical Psychologist* (1935; 2d ed. 1936). A vigorous essay, wholly on Freud's wavelength, by an English analyst whom Freud highly respected.

Freud, Martin. *Sigmund Freud: Man and Father* (1958). A charming and revealing memoir.

Freud, Sigmund. "Zur Psychologie des Gymnasiasten" (1914), *GW* X, 204–07 / "Some Reflections on Schoolboy Psychology," *SE* XIII, 241–44. Revealing reminiscences which Freud, in his usual way, takes as an incentive for generalization.

Gay, Peter. "Six Names in Search of an Interpretation: A Contribution to the Debate over Sigmund Freud's Jewishness." *Hebrew Union College Annual,* LIII (1982), 295–307.

———. *Freud: A Life for Our Time* (forthcoming 1988).

Gilman, Sander. *Jewish Self-Hatred: Anti-Semitism and the Hidden Language of the Jews* (1986). Thoughtful, at times I think overstated, reflections on a vital theme; I found the pages on Freud's language and jokes (250–69 passim) less than persuasive.

Ginsburg, Solomon W. *Man's Place in God's World: A Psychiatric Evaluation* (1948). A relatively sympathetic interpretation by a theologian.

Graf, Max. "Reminiscences of Professor Sigmund Freud." *Psychoanalytic Quarterly,* XI (1942), 465–76. Telling, by no means worshipful comments on the Freud of the Wednesday Psychological Society years.

Grinstein, Alexander. *On Sigmund Freud's Dreams* (1968). An important survey.

Grollman, Earl A. *Judaism in Sigmund Freud's World* (1965). A brave, modest, scarcely original attempt to define Freud's Jewishness and assess its influence on his work; characteristic of a growing literature.

Guirdham, Arthur. *Christ and Freud: A Study of Religious Experience and Observance* (1959). As a psychiatrist and vitalist, Guirdham attempts to refute Freud on religion.

Hammond, Guyton B. *Man in Estrangement: A Comparison of the Thought of Paul Tillich and Erich Fromm* (1965). Helpful for both.

Hughes, Thomas Hywel. *Psychology and Religious Origins* (1936). A characteristic product by a modern divine, seeking to expound

Freud fairly, but convinced that he "treats religion with a studied indifference" (p. 33); "studied contempt" would have come closer to the truth.

Hull, David L. *Darwin and His Critics: The Reception of Darwin's Theory of Evolution by the Scientific Community* (1973). A rich anthology testifying to the complex response to Darwin's ideas, with an illuminating introduction.

Jones, Peter d'A. *The Christian Socialist Revival, 1877–1914: Religion, Class, and Social Conscience in Late-Victorian England* (1968). A dependable and informative monograph.

Klein, Dennis B. *Jewish Origins of the Psychoanalytic Movement* (1981). Though I find Klein's thesis, summarized in the title, unacceptable, I have found much of value in his material.

Krüll, Marianne. *Freud and His Father* (1979; tr. Arnold J. Pomerans, 1986). Thorough research into Freud's family background; it well summarizes recent scholarship. I am skeptical about some of her interpretations.

LaBarre, Weston. *The Ghost Dance: The Origins of Religion* (1970). A brilliant, sweeping, combative psychoanalytic account of religion from its prehistoric beginnings as the great cultural neurosis.

Loewenberg, Peter. "'Sigmund Freud as a Jew': A Study in Ambivalence and Courage." *Journal of the History of the Behavioral Sciences,* VII (1971), 363–69. Tersely but interestingly explores the familiar texts (Freud's letters, reminiscences, and public statements) to arrive at conclusions somewhat at variance from my own.

———. "A Hidden Zionist Theme in Freud's 'My Son the Myops' Dream." *Journal of the History of Ideas,* XXXI (1971), 129–31. Traces Freud's pro-Zionist leanings through one of his recorded dreams.

Loewenstein, Rudolph. *Christians and Jews: A Psychoanalytic Study* (1951). A leading ego psychologist attempting to explain anti-Semitism.

McClelland, David C. *Psychoanalysis and Religious Mysticism,* a pamphlet of 1959. The psychologist known for his espousal of the "achievement motive" here speaks of the "unconscious religious assumptions of psychoanalysis" (4). Freud's psychoanalysis, he holds, "is not overtly a religious movement. . . . But whatever its conscious intentions, as a *social movement* its functions are much broader than these. Its leading practitioners have charisma: they are looked up to, admired and treated as beyond the ordinary run of humanity in much the same way as ministers and priests have been at various times in the past." Its "metaphysics" are "seriously discussed," much like "theological questions. . . . Above all it *heals* and we should not forget that one of the basic and most fundamental appeals of Christianity as described in the New Testament was its healing power. At least on the surface then—and the idea is by no means original with me—psychoanalysis has many of the characteristics of a religious movement" (5). At least the disclaimer of originality we may take seriously. It is a measure of this appraisal that it highly values David Bakan's "remarkable" book showing Freud's dependence on the Jewish mystical tradition (7). (For Bakan, see above, 130–31.)

McGrath, William J. *Freud's Discovery of Psychoanalysis: The Politics of Hysteria* (1986). A civilized, scholarly, highly informative study of Freud's intellectual development but somewhat compromised by its thesis that psychoanalysis is a kind of "counterpolitics."

Michaelis, Edgar. *Die Menschheitsproblematik der Freudschen Psychoanalyse* (1925). Critical but not unappreciative pamphlet by a nerve specialist in Berlin.

Miller, Justin. "Interpretations of Freud's Jewishness, 1924–1974." *Journal of the History of the Behavioral Sciences*, XVII (1981), 357–74. Satisfactorily summarizes half a century of writings. His readings, to the extent we overlap, tend to agree with mine.

Money-Kyrle, Roger. *Superstition and Society* (1939). A series of lectures to the Institute of Psycho-Analysis by an English analyst trying to make Freud's ideas on religion more digestible.

Myers, Gerald E. *William James: His Life and Thought* (1986). Exhaustive.

Oldfield, John J. "The Evolution of Lammenais' Catholic-Liberal Synthesis." *Journal for the Scientific Study of Religion,* VIII (1969), 269–88. Valuable for an account of liberal Roman Catholicism in early-nineteenth-century France.

Oring, Elliott. *The Jokes of Sigmund Freud: A Study in Humor and Jewish Identity* (1984). Though with some suggestive ideas, this grave study tends to overinterpret Freud's humor.

Ostow, Mortimer, ed. *Judaism and Psychoanalysis* (1982). A collection of essays of varying merit. See esp. Martin S. Bergmann above.

Ostow, Mortimer, and Ben-Ami Scharfstein. *The Need to Believe* (1954). Psychoanalytic reflections.

Petuchowski, Jakob J. "Erich Fromm's Midrash on Love: The Sacred and the Secular Forms." *Commentary,* XXII (December 1956), 543–49. A learned commentary on Fromm's *The Art of Loving.*

Pfrimmer, Theo. *Freud: Lecteur de la Bible* (1982). A useful, very bulky study of Freud's reading in the sacred texts, pursued chronologically.

Pruyser, Paul W. *A Dynamic Psychology of Religion* (1968). A systematic, most interesting overview and theory of religious psychology.

———. "Sigmund Freud and His Legacy: Psychoanalytic Psychology of Religion." In *Beyond the Classics? Essays in the Scientific Study of Religion* (1973), edited by Charles Y. Glock and Phillip E. Hammond, 243–90. An excellent, informative, and suggestive survey.

Rainey, Reuben B. *Freud as a Student of Religion: Perspectives on the Background and Development of His Thought* (1975). A scholarly study, emphasizing Freud's religious education in his school years.

Rawidowicz, Simon. *Ludwig Feuerbachs Philosophie. Ursprung und Schicksal* (1931). A good monograph with several useful pages on Feuerbach and Freud.

Reik, Theodor. *Ritual: Psycho-Analytic Studies* (1928; tr. from the second German edition by Douglas Bryan, 1931). A characteristic series of papers on religion, including studies on the Shofar and Kol Nidre, from a severe Freudian perspective, blessed by Freud himself with a preface.

————. *From Thirty Years with Freud* (tr. Richard Winston, 1940). Intimate reminiscences, and a chapter (XI) on Jewish humor and the tragedies it covers over.

————. *Jewish Wit* (1962). On Freud's jokes.

Rieff, Philip. *Freud: The Mind of the Moralist* (1959). A thoughtful and substantial essay, with some fine pages on Freud and the Enlightenment (see esp. 286–87).

Rizzuto, Ana-Maria. *The Birth of the Living God: A Psychoanalytic Study* (1979). A fascinating monograph, based on rich clinical materials, of how patients represent the divinity to themselves.

Robertson, J. M. *Explorations* (n.d.). Several severe and lucid critiques of religious thought, including two unrespectful but highly convincing papers entitled "Professor James's Plea for Theism" and "Professor James on Religious Experience."

Rosenberg, Ann Elizabeth. *Freudian Theory and American Religious Journals, 1900–1965* (1980). A somewhat stodgy but helpful survey.

Rosmarin, Trude Weiss. *The Hebrew Moses: An Answer to Sigmund Freud* (1939). An angry pamphlet.

Rothman, Stanley, and Phillip Isenberg. "Sigmund Freud and the Politics of Marginality." *Central European History,* VII (March 1974), 58–78. A persuasive discussion; helps to undermine the Schorske-McGrath thesis (see under both names).

Rubenstein, Richard. *The Religious Imagination: A Study in Psychoanalysis and Jewish Theology* (1968).

Sachs, Hanns. *Freud, Master and Friend* (1945). A valuable brief memoir by a close disciple; its pages on Vienna Jewry are rewarding.

Schaar, John H. *Escape from Authority: The Perspectives of Erich Fromm* (1961).

Schoenwald, Richard. *Freud: The Man and His Mind* (1956). Stresses Freud's Jewishness.

Schorske, Carl. "Politics and Patricide in Freud's Interpretation of Dreams." *American Historical Review,* LXXVIII (April 1973), 328–47, republished in *Fin-de-Siècle Vienna* (1980), 181–207. Originated the thesis that Freud developed psychoanalysis as a response to the untoward political situation in Vienna.

Schur, Max. *Freud: Living and Dying* (1972). An important biographical study by Freud's last physician including comments on his Jewishness.

Sealfeld, Hans. *Das Christentum in der Beleuchtung der Psychoanalyse* (1928). Criticizes Pfister for his "alliance" with Freud.

Selbie, W. B. *The Fatherhood of God* (1936). A study by a doctor of divinity firmly arguing that "the psychological explanation of the Fatherhood of God as arising out of needs felt most acutely in childhood is insufficient and inadequate" (p. 14).

Shengold, Leonard. "Freud and Joseph." In *The Unconscious Today: Essays in Honor of Max Schur,* edited by Mark Kanzer (1971), 473–94. A most interesting paper on Freud's multiple identifications with Josephs all his life.

Siegman, Aron Wolfe. "An Empirical Investigation of the Psychoanalytic Theory of Religious Behavior." *Journal for the Scientific Study of Religion,* I (October 1961), 74–78. Slight but suggestive: finds some positive correlations to Freud's theories but is unconvinced.

Simon, Ernst. "Sigmund Freud, the Jew." In *Leo Baeck Institute Yearbook* II (1957), 270–305. A pioneering and encyclopedic, not completely flawless, effort to which much later discussion has been indebted.

Spiro, Melford E. "Religious Systems as Culturally Constituted Defense Mechanisms." In *Context and Meaning in Cultural Anthropology,* edited by M. E. Spiro (1965).

———. "Symbolism and Functionalism in the Anthropological Study of Religion." In *Science of Religion. Studies in Methodology,* Proceedings of the Study Conference of the International Association for the History of Religions, held in Turku, Finland, August 27–31, 1973 (1973), edited by Lauri Honko, 322–93.

———. "Culture and Human Nature." In *The Making of Psychological Anthropology,* edited by George D. Spindler (1978), 330–60. These three titles are only a sampling of the stimulating papers on the theme of religion by a cultural anthropologist who knows his Freud and uses him well.

Stokes, Allison. *Ministry after Freud* (1985).

Strout, Cushing. "The Pluralistic Identity of William James: A Psychohistorical Reading of *The Varieties of Religious Experience.*" *American Quarterly,* XXIII (May 1971). A revealing essay by a psychoanalytically oriented intellectual historian.

Thouless, Robert H. *An Introduction to the Psychology of Religion* (1924). Typical of many such titles published in Freud's lifetime, critical of the psychoanalytic "reduction of the doctrines of religion to fulfilments of human wishes with the implicit conclusion that they are therefore illusory" (p. 264).

Thwaite, Ann. *Edmund Gosse: A Literary Landscape, 1849–1928* (1984). A full and civilized biography.

Weatherhead, Leslie D. *Psychology in the Service of the Soul* (1929). A Methodist's plea for cooperation between psychologists and theologians.

———. *Psychology, Religion, and Healing* (1951; rev. ed., 1955). A thoroughgoing historical survey of all types of religious healing, with a chapter on Freud and another denying that religious experience is a neurosis.

Weinstein, Jacob J. "Religion Looks at Psychiatry." *Pastoral Psychology,* IX (November 1958), 25–32. Suggests that Reform rabbis have little problem in using psychiatry in the cure of souls, but the psychiatry he has in mind is the "Revisionist" wing of Erich Fromm and allies.

Wellisch, E. *Isaac and Oedipus. A Study in Biblical Psychology of the Sacrifice of Isaac. The Akedah* (1954). Plea, by an English physician, for a "Biblical psychology."

Worcester, Elwood, Samuel McComb, and Isador H. Coriat. *Religion and Medicine: The Moral Control of Nervous Disorders* (1908). A curious and fascinating collaborative effort between two divines and one physician (Coriat), who later became one of the first converts to psychoanalysis in the United States.

INDEX

Abraham, Karl, 78, 120, 121, 131
Amsel, Avrohom, 97
Anglicanism, 9
Atheism: in the nineteenth century, 6–9, 11, 12–14; among scientists, 9, 29; among psychoanalysts, 45, 104–05; in Enlightenment, 46, 49–50, 62, 66–67. *See also* Freud; Religion

Bacon, Francis, 51
Bakan, David, 130
Bakhtin, Mikhail, 39
Balmary, Marie, 58*n*
Baruk, Henri, 131
Bebel, August, 11
Biblical criticism, 46
Biddle, W. Earl, 92–93
Binswanger, Ludwig, 56, 143
Blavatsky, Madame Elena, 14
Bleuler, Eugen, 145
Bonaparte, Princess Marie, 12, 151
Brentano, Franz, 38, 60
Breuer, Josef, 128, 139
Brierley, Marjorie, 107–09
Brucke, Ernst, 42, 60–62
Buber, Martin, 96, 100, 149

Cabbalism, 130
Catholicism. *See* Roman Catholicism
Censorship, 43–45
Charcot, Jean-Martin, 41*n*
Christian Science, 14

Christian Socialism, 10–11
Christians and Christianity: views of Freud, 40, 57–58, 71–72, 81–95; Freud's views, 44–45, 59; psychoanalysts and adherents, 73–80, 86–90, 92–95, 108–12. *See also* Religion; Roman Catholicism
Condillac, abbé de, 52, 63
Copernicus, 64

Darwin, Charles, 60, 140–43, 144, 146, 147
Darwinism, 24, 59, 64
Deism, 66
Diderot, Denis, 45, 49–50
Draper, John William, 6, 14, 15
Du Bois-Reymond, Emil, 60, 62

Eder, M. D., 132
Ehrenwald, Hans, 131
Eitingon, Max, 12, 77, 79, 123, 150
Ellis, Havelock, 41*n*
Engels, Friedrich, 13, 53
England, religion in, 10, 13, 14
Enlightenment: Freud's attitude toward, 41–44, 50, 62; censorship in, 43–44; atheism in, 46, 49–50, 62, 66–67; and philosophy, 50–53, 62–63
Existentialism, 90

Ferenczi, Sándor, 111, 134, 143
Feuchtwang, David, 119–20

179

Feuerbach, Ludwig, 53–56
Fliess, Wilhelm, 18, 61, 77, 78
France, anticlericalism in, 7, 9, 11
Franzblau, Abraham N., 100n, 103n
French Revolution, 8
Freud, Amalia, 125
Freud, Anna, 143, 144; on Judaism,
    118–19; quoted, 22n, 76, 82n
Freud, Ernst, 126
Freud, Harry, 3–4
Freud, Jacob, and Judaism, 8, 125
Freud, Martha, 153
Freud, Martin, 125, 126
Freud, Sigmund:
—his atheism: in biographies, 3–4; his
    statements, 3–4, 12, 33–34, 37–38,
    47–48, 56, 65, 68, 79–81, 111, 112,
    127, 153–54; and psychoanalytic the-
    ory, 30–31, 37, 41, 45–48, 63–65,
    67, 108–09, 146–49; viewed by
    Marxists, 39–40; viewed by Chris-
    tians, 40, 57–58, 71–72, 81–95,
    108–12; and the Enlightenment, 41–
    44, 50, 62; and medicine, 42, 59,
    60–61; psychoanalyzed, 56–59, 150;
    viewed by Jews, 72, 95–104, 130–31,
    149–50, 152
—and religion: and science, 4–5, 17–18,
    24, 28, 32, 43, 44–50, 59, 66, 80,
    150–54; explanations for religious feel-
    ing, 11–12, 17, 23, 40–41, 136; re-
    ligious metaphors, 17–19, 96–97,
    143; adolescence, 20n, 103n; com-
    pared to James, 21–24, 26, 27, 28,
    30, 68; and telepathy, 22, 148; and
    literature, 33, 129; self-censorship,
    44; attitude toward Christianity, 44–
    45, 59; philosophy and theology, 53,
    55–56; and religious psychoanalysts,
    73–80, 106–07; Jewish self-identifi-
    cation, 121–27, 129–34, 136–39,
    146, 148, 151–52; Jewish religious
    behavior, 124–27, 130–31, 153; in-
    tellectual struggles, 143–46; and fe-
    male sexuality, 151

—works: *The Future of an Illusion*, 12,
    31, 41, 46–47, 48, 65, 72, 79, 120,
    130, 153–54; *New Introductory Lectures
    on Psychoanalysis*, 47; *The Interpretation
    of Dreams*, 59, 78; *Civilization and Its
    Discontents*, 68; "Obsessive Acts and
    Religious Practices," 73; *Totem and Ta-
    boo*, 96, 105, 126, 133, 134, 152;
    Moses and Monotheism, 112, 149–50,
    152
—correspondence: Bonaparte, 12, 151;
    Eitingon, 12, 77, 79, 123; Martha
    Bernays, 18; Fliess, 18, 78; Silber-
    stein, 38, 60; Zweig, 65; Abraham,
    78, 120, 121, 131; Pfister, 81–82,
    86–87, 107, 111; Jung, 83, 143;
    Jones, 105, 148; Ferenczi, 111, 134;
    Singer, 112; Jaffe, 123
—*See also* Psychoanalysis
Fromm, Erich, 100, 105–07

Gambetta, Leon, 9
Garbett, Cyril Forster, 87
Gibbon, Edward, 67
Gladstone, William, 21
Gosse, Edmund, 8, 21

Haeckel, Ernst, 7
Hammerschlag, Samuel, 124
Hart, Bernard, 20n
Heller, Hugo, 129
Helmholtz, Hermann, 18, 60, 61
Hoffer, Willi, 74
Hume, David, 51
Huxley, T. H., 6–7, 60, 141

Ibsen, Henrik, 137

Jaffe, L., 123
James, William, 108; studies of religion,
    7, 14, 21–30, 48, 67–68; compared
    to Freud, 21–24, 26, 27, 28, 30, 68;
    The Will to Believe, 22; *The Varieties of
    Religious Experience*, 25
Jenkin, Fleeming, 142

Jews and Judaism: in nineteenth century, 9; attitudes of, toward Freud, 72, 95–104, 117, 130–31, 149–50, 152; psychoanalysts and adherents, 77–78, 96n, 99–105, 117–22, 134–35, 137–39, 145–46; analysands, 117–18, 128–29, 135–36, 139; Freud's self-identification, 121–27, 129–34, 136–39, 146, 148, 151–52; Freud's religious behavior, 124–27, 130–31, 153. See also Religion

Jones, Ernest, 20n, 44–45, 61n, 68, 104–05, 135, 138; Freud's relationship to, 143; correspondence with Freud, 148

Jung, Carl: Freud's attitude toward, 75–76, 77, 78, 120, 121, 143; correspondence with Freud, 83, 143; attitude toward religion, 118, 120

Kaplan, Mordecai, 72
Karr, Alphonse, 20
Katz, Robert L., 95
Kautsky, Karl, 39–40
Keren Hajessod, 123
Klein, Joel, 97–98
Klein, Melanie, 143
Krass, Nathan, 72
Kushner, Martin, 96–97

La Bletterie, abbé de, 67
Lammenais, abbé de, 9–10
Lee, R. S., 93–95, 108
Leibniz, 66
Liebman, Joshua Loth, 100–04
Locke, John, 66–67
Love, 73, 83–85, 94, 106. See also Psychoanalysis
Lueger, Karl, 138
Lyell, Charles, 60

McDougall, William, 117–18
Marr, G. Simpson, 88
Marx, Karl, 17, 105
Marxism, and Freud, 17, 39

Meissner, W. W., 57, 111–12
Meynert, Theodor, 42
Morselli, Enrico, 127

Nathansohn, Amalia. See Freud, Amalia
Naumann, Friedrich, 10
Newton, Isaac, 43, 51–52, 63
Niebuhr, Reinhold, 71, 91
Nothnagel, Hermann, 42

Pfister, Oskar, 20, 37, 41, 46–47, 67, 73–75; relationship with Freud, 74–87, 100, 106, 112, 143; correspondence with Freud, 81–82, 86–87, 107, 111

Philosophy: Enlightenment, 50–53; and Freud, 53, 55–56; nineteenth century, 53–55. See also Religion

Philp, H. C., 19–20
Pietism, 85
Piper, Otto A., 92
Pius IX, Pope, 10, 109
Psychoanalysis: as religion, 19–21, 31–33; and atheism, 45, 104–05; scientific status, 47, 63–65, 67, 145; religious adherents, 73–80, 86–90, 92–95, 96n, 99–104, 105–12; Jewishness, 117–22, 127–35, 137–39, 145–48. See also Freud

Putnam, James Jackson, 110–11

Rank, Otto, 143
Religion: conflict with science, 4–7, 11, 12–17, 24–30, 32, 43, 45–50, 55–56, 66–68, 94; in nineteenth century, 7–17; psychoanalytic explanations, 11–12, 17, 23, 40–41, 136; psychoanalysis as, 19–21, 31–33; science as, 20–21, 23–24, 31–32; for James, 21–30. See also Atheism; Christianity; Freud

Roback, A. A., 117, 130, 132n, 135
Robert, Marthe, 58n
Roberts, Henry L., 20
Rolland, Romain, 17, 134

Roman Catholicism, 84–85; in nineteenth century, 9–10, 11, 15; attitude toward Freudianism, 40, 44, 109, 111–12; Freud's attitude toward, 59. *See also* Christianity
Rosenberg, Stuart E., 98–99
Rosenzweig, Franz, 96

Sadger, Isidor, 135
Schwaber, Paul, 118–19*n*
Science: conflict with religion, 4–7, 11, 12–17, 24–30, 32, 43, 45–50, 55–56, 66–68, 94; psychoanalysis as, 19–21, 31–33; as religion, 20–21, 23–24, 31–32; philosophy of, 46, 53. *See also* Darwin; Enlightenment; Psychoanalysis
Secularism, 4–11, 14
Silber, Abba Hillel, 99*n*
Silberstein, Eduard, 38, 60
Singer, Charles, 112
Spinoza, Baruch (Benedict), 46
Steinberg, Milton, 96*n*

Stekel, Wilhelm, 120–21
Strachey, James, 47

Theology, 54. *See also* Philosophy; Religion
Theosophy, 14
Theresa, Saint, 25
Tillich, Paul, 88–90
Tournier, Paul, 91
Turgot, Anne-Robert-Jacques, 63
Tyndall, John, 60

Virchow, Rudolf, 60
Voltaire (François Arouet), 43, 49, 67

White, Andrew Dickson, 6, 16
Whitman, Walt, 25

Zilboorg, Gregory, 57–58, 109–10
Zinzendorf, Count, 85
Zola, Emile, 136
Zweig, Arnold, 147, 150, 152
Zweig, Stefan, 65